ADVANCE PRAISE FOR
FEAR LESS, LIVE MORE

'This book is full of wisdom from an amazing human. Aimee Fuller is triple-distilled, 100% positivity, passion and inspiration. Anyone you know facing physical and mental challenges will find wisdom and advice among her great stories.'
Dr Xand van Tulleken

'I love how Aimee smashes through life conquering any fears that stand in her way. *Fear Less, Live More* is a must read for anyone who wants to live life to the full.'
Jade Jones OBE

'Aimee's treatment of fear is real, raw, relatable and uplifting.'
Wayne Bridge

FEAR LESS, LIVE MORE

FEAR LESS,
LIVE MORE

Everything I've learned
from testing my limits

AIMEE FULLER

ASTER*

First published in Great Britain in 2022 by Aster, an imprint of
Octopus Publishing Group Ltd
Carmelite House
50 Victoria Embankment
London EC4Y 0DZ
www.octopusbooks.co.uk

An Hachette UK Company
www.hachette.co.uk

Text copyright © Aimee Fuller 2022

ISBN: 978-1-78325-411-8

A CIP catalogue record for this book is available from the British Library.

Typeset in 11/17pt Cardo by Jouve (UK), Milton Keynes

Printed and bound in Great Britain by Clays Ltd, Elcograf S.p.A.

10 9 8 7 6 5 4 3 2 1

Co-author: Carl Hindmarch

Senior commissioning editor: Natalie Bradley
Copyeditor: Caroline Blake
Art director: Yasia Williams-Leedham
Production manager: Caroline Alberti

This FSC® label means that materials used for the
product have been responsibly sourced.

To my Grandad Paul, lucky number 6, always
and for ever. This one's for you.

And to Nelson Pratt, always in our hearts,
our snowboard coach and mentor.

Pump with the calm, ride on Nelly!

CONTENTS

INTRODUCTION

Outside your comfort zone is a dangerous place to be. It's scary, but it can also be fun. It's somewhere I've spent most of my life. In fact, I made a career out of it. As a professional snowboarder, my sporting career involved throwing myself very fast down an icy slope on a thin piece of plywood and then turning myself upside-down a couple of times halfway down a mountain. It wasn't a bad choice for a career. I got to travel the world, hang with some of the loveliest people on the planet and compete in the Olympics twice. Most people wouldn't even call snowboarding work. I have to admit, most of the time it was a blast.

Yet there were other times when I thought, *this isn't fun*. There were moments when I wanted to stop the ride and get off. Throwing myself off a jump when it was -40 degrees and I wasn't sure if I'd quite got the trick right was when my love of the sport turned to hate. I hated it and I was afraid. When things go wrong, they really go wrong.

Snowboarding isn't forgiving. I've lost friends to the sport I fell in love with all those years ago, but I would strive not to think about that and start that negative thought process when I was competing. The dangers of the sport are exactly why snowboarders don't talk about fear. We're certainly not meant to feel it. Like most athletes, we're meant to be trained robots trying to process this thing, compartmentalize it and not allow it to interfere with our performance. But we do feel it. The deep, stomach-turning, sick-in-the-back-of-the-mouth fear that hammers on your chest and shouts, *if I get this wrong, I will injure myself.* Athletes aren't some special breed of humanity made in a secret factory. We're regular people and along with the other 99.9 per cent of human beings on the planet, every single one of us knows fear and has to deal with it every day of our lives.

What even is fear? How does it work and how can we make it our friend? For me, it is a form of dialogue. It's about respecting an unknown territory. Dealing with fear on and off the slopes was my job. Some lessons I was taught, some I worked out for myself, others I'm still working on. The modest ambition of this book is to share these life experiences with you, so that you can deal with difficult situations in your own life. Fear has driven, inspired and helped me; I believe it can do the same for you.

Sometimes, fear can be debilitating and impair your ability to function. Knowing how to distinguish between adrenaline-inducing anxiety and overwhelming fear can be the difference between success and failure. Even life and death. Anxiety is one of the most difficult emotions to decipher, especially when you are trying to make a change in your life. By definition, being outside your comfort zone will make you feel some discomfort or anxiety. But this kind of discomfort is also a prerequisite for growth.

People often say that if you are working to achieve a positive goal, you should push through the anxiety that arises as you move outside your comfort zone. The idea is that if you push yourself through, you will get past it and achieve your goal. Sorted! The problem is, that only works if you actually achieve the final goal. What if you don't? Sometimes you push outside your comfort zone and land on your face (literally, in my case). This can reinforce your fears, or even create new ones. These are the experiences I want to share with you – the times when I have been closest to fear, my worst anxieties realized – because that is when I've learned the most about myself and what I want from life. I want to help you realize what is most important to you and I want to help you grab it with both hands. You will get to know your fears, celebrate your strengths, learn from your failures and visualize your successes. More than anything, I hope this book offers you an attitude.

1

ONE FEAR TO RULE THEM ALL

You only get two jumps at the Olympics Big Air event and I've missed the final practice. Feeling cold and a little bit flustered, I'm running a dialogue with myself that goes something like, *Okay, Aimee, this is not ideal, but it doesn't matter. Just get on with it. You've done it before, you can do it again. It is what it is. Don't let this feeling consume you, don't let it define you, don't let it be you. Shit. Aimee, get your head in the game. This is the Olympics!* I convinced myself that I'd be fine because sometimes, as I like to tell myself, I'm better when I'm not prepared.

I'm at the top of jump one of two, trying to work out which way I am going to heel-toe, flat-based 'bam' before I drop in. The flat-based 'bam' bit is the point at which I'm set to explode off the jump to initiate the manoeuvre. I drop in, still cold and flustered, but I manage to get it. I do the 180, the double backflip, and land both feet on the ground. Then I fall down. Flat on my arse. I just think, *shit*. If I had landed this without falling down, the doors of opportunity would have opened. Now, I could feel them close. *Fuck. What now?* I feel a mental pain that could eat me alive.

*

Fear is known to cause physiological changes and ultimately behavioural changes, such as freezing, fighting or panicking at perceived traumatic events. Or, as my mate says, freeze, fight or fuck. It's an innate response to coping with danger. It works by accelerating the breathing and heart rate, while constricting the peripheral blood vessels. This leads to blushing, increases muscle tension and causes the muscles attached to each hair follicle to contract, prompting goosebumps, which make a cold person warmer or a frightened animal look more impressive. It causes sweating, as well as increasing levels of glucose and white blood cells. This raises alertness, leading to sleep disturbance and butterflies in the stomach. With all of these physiological changes at play, our consciousness realizes an emotion: fear.

Don't get me wrong. Fear was always there in my career, from very early on. I had just masked it really well. If I had properly thought about the importance and pressure around the Olympics, and let that define me, I would have been a wreck. For the most part, I managed to trick myself into believing it was just another day in my life. It was just a competition, with all the people I normally competed against – with a few more spectators. I always had at the back of my mind the idea that most of life's defining events were not in fact what defined you. You could always have another go. Try again. That's how I dealt with it. That's what I did. Plus, I was only 26 – relatively young to be doing what I was doing – and I felt I had the rest of my life ahead of me if things didn't work out. I loved the opportunities snowboarding had given me, but I always felt I wasn't going to ride competitively for ever.

Out of some 26 other possible feelings (trust me, I counted them), fear is unique in its ability to have an immediate physical effect on us. It makes us *feel* something else. We can't *not* feel it. More than that, it makes us *do* things and, at an innate gut level, fear does things to us. It's

7

involuntary. Fear is a vital response to physical and emotional danger and has been pivotal throughout our evolution. This primitive mechanism helped humans survive by either running away from or fighting a perceived danger. It's there from birth as the startle response in babies and it stays with us. If human beings didn't feel fear, they wouldn't have been able to protect themselves from legitimate threats, which often had life-or-death consequences in the ancestral world. Sabre-tooth tigers, woolly mammoths, marauding Neanderthals. A fight-or-flight impulse was super-handy 20,000 years ago as a life-preservation tool.

In the modern world, the stakes are generally lower. Although public speaking, elevators and spiders generally don't present life-or-death consequences, some individuals still develop extreme fight, flight or freeze responses to specific objects or scenarios. Many people experience bouts of fear, such as when they're giving a high-stakes presentation, or feelings of nerves, for example, when they are going on a first date. Heart-stopping moments in horror films trigger the same automatic fight-or-flight response, lighting up our synapses like a pinball machine, flooding our brain with hormonal responses that trigger physiological reactions. But when a fear is persistent, specific to a certain threat and impairs one's life or growth, that is when it has become a specific phobia.

People live in fear of what has happened, what might happen or indeed could happen again. For most of us, fear is actually the anxiety around something that hasn't happened. The fear of an unknown future event. The fear of the future. What if my boyfriend or girlfriend leaves me? What if I get an illness or lose my job? What if a family member dies? Then there's the fear of an unexpected event, for example, my big fear of having a snowboard accident. I always thought that if I broke my neck, the fear was less about my own welfare and more about how it would impact my mum and dad. Scientists have studied fear for years, but recently a new theory has emerged of how fear works and how all the fearful feelings we have really boil down to one thing: fear of the unknown.

Fear of what might happen tomorrow. Or the next day. It's the fear of opening a door and walking into a room full of strangers. It's the fear of what's about to happen when you have to do the thing you are afraid of. In ten minutes. In five. Right now. Rationally I always used to say that these are fears I should choose not to live with. I try to live as presently as possible. When bad things happen, I try to deal with them and move on. Fear of the future is imaginary. It hasn't happened, so what's to be afraid of, right? But in practice it's not that easy. Writing in the *Journal of Anxiety Disorders* in 2016, Professor R N Carleton reviewed current research on fear and anxiety and came up with the theory that all human fears, from snakes to failure, boil down to one thing. According to the prof, all our fears are really just forms of anxiety about the future. The one fear to rule them all.

This could not be more true of my first experience of the Olympics in Sochi, Russia in 2014. I didn't know what it would be like or what *I* would be like there. Would I be good enough? What if I arrived and was out of my depth? What if I hurt myself before the competition and had to pull out? There were so many unknowns that I found myself playing the whole thing down in my head – *yeah, I guess it would be cool if I could go to Sochi, I wouldn't mind that* – because I didn't feel in control of the outcome. I was scared that committing to this goal meant risking failure.

I had a totally different experience of fear the second time around. On the road to the PyeongChang Olympics in South Korea, I knew what I wanted, and nothing could stop me from getting there. By 2018, my mentality was: *this is what I want, this is what I'll do, this is how I will get there.* I knew that the way to get there was to be 100 per cent committed to every opportunity that came my way. I was no longer afraid of reaching for my goal. Learning how to deal with these fears and assembling a bag of tricks and life hacks meant that I brought a heap of knowledge about what it was I was afraid of.

What I didn't know was that it was going to get a lot more gnarly on the road to the second Olympics. That it would test and challenge me in ways I could never have predicted and, despite all the mental resilience I had developed, the journey would be so much more painful. What's really interesting is that I felt less fear going into it, but I would soon experience a kind of fear that I had never felt before. A fear that would ultimately overwhelm me.

2

GETTING TO KNOW FEAR

When I was three or four, my dad bought me a 14-foot trampoline. It was the *crème de la crème* of super-tramps, a big square one. Straight away, my mum was like, 'Oh, no, no, no, the kids can't have that', so it got sent back. Six months later, there was a 50cc quad bike in the garden. It was fun, but it wasn't fast enough for me, so it got upgraded to a motocross bike. At age six, motocross was my first experience of feeling a pure adrenaline rush: the sound of the engine, the smell of petrol, the deep breath on the start line. The fear.

Down the line, left and right, bike to bike, eight-year-old boys would be sticking their elbows in front of me because they didn't want to get beaten by a girl. Later, I'd see some of the boys walking around with broken arms, broken collarbones. Danny Webb is now a world-famous championship rider, but back in the day I broke his collarbone. We took off at the same time, elbow to elbow, and he wiped out. (If you're reading this now, sorry, Danny!) It is crazy how little inhibition I had as a child. I would go skiing with my brother Josh at our local dry ski slope and I remember us going from the top to the bottom as fast as we could, just to see how far we could get up the stop ramp, across the grass matting and over the concrete to touch the wooden ski hut. As a kid, I dabbled in everything: gymnastics, motocross, lacrosse. I was good at all of them, but I didn't excel at any of them, until later when my dad said, 'You're good at so many sports, but if you invest your energy into one you really like, you never know, you could turn it into something bigger.'

I discovered snowboarding when I was living in America. My family moved there when I was 12 years old and it was the first time I had experienced an emotional setback. When we first moved I hated it there so much I used to get on the school bus crying. At that age, friends mean more than anything. (Steph, my best friend from England, came out to visit twice, which shows the level of friendship we had and how much I missed England.) Then I met my friends Tareq Alhegelan, Oli Staunton and Carly

Burns; we went snowboarding together and suddenly that became my lifeline. Snowboarding broke the mould for me in comparison to the other sports. There were no rules. There was room for creativity. There was no stopwatch. No one was watching you or telling you what to do. You're on the mountain, having an adventure with your friends and that is the absolute core of what snowboarding is about.

I was 15 when I heard about High Cascade Snowboard Camp on Mount Hood, Oregon. I took a flyer from school, stuffed it under my mum's nose, and kept going on and on about it until eventually my parents agreed to pay for it as a birthday present. The camp took place over six days, but I actually only spent five days there because I missed my flight. I was so nervous about flying that I went to McDonald's to distract myself and sat at the gate with my headphones in, trying to look cool. The problem was, I thought you were meant to get on the plane at the time it said on the ticket. No one told me that's the time the plane takes off, so I was eating my McDonald's breakfast while the plane left me behind.

When I finally got to camp, I was so excited. It was the end of July, my birthday. My previous experience of snowboarding was just a few days here and there during the winter in Pennsylvania and Virginia. When you arrive at the camp, you fill in a form to estimate your level, what experience you've got and what tricks you can do, that sort of thing. I was classed as beginner to intermediate. I met up with Gretchen Bleiler, who was the guest pro on the camp. I remember every time I saw her on the mountain, the excitement of seeing a real-life pro, I just used to stare at her. I was so in awe and I have very vivid memories of every time she dropped into our group to ride.

I remember there was another pro alongside Gretchen and, as sponsored athletes, they got tons of gear and stuff, so the riders gave it away. It's the coolest thing you can imagine to get a free snowboard. There was a little competition at the end of the camp. Basically, whoever ran around the whole campsite fastest would win the snowboard. I remember thinking *I have to win this.* There were boys and girls of all different ages. They shouted, 'Go!' and I have never run so fast in my life. It must have been about 1,500 metres and I gave it absolutely everything. I came in first and was elated. I had Gretchen sign the board and it was just the best thing ever.

The following year I really wanted to go back to camp but it wasn't part of the plan. Mum had planned our first skiing holiday in America. My parents had saved up; it was a really big thing and their way of supporting me. We went to Breckenridge, Colorado for a week and I broke my collarbone on day one. That was my first snowboarding injury and it really changed my attitude to fear.

In hindsight, I probably got hurt for a very good reason! I was trying to hit this really gnarly rail. Even now I question why I even wanted to do it. But I didn't have any experience, I didn't recognize the danger in it. Ignorance may be bliss, but if you don't know what the dangers are you will end up hurting yourself. Before that, I'd felt pretty much untouchable. This was the most important lesson of them all. I realized in that instant, that specific moment, that I wasn't invincible.

As children we are all pretty fearless. It's the grown-ups who often show us what fear is: the look on their face when we run away in a supermarket, their reaction when we fall over, and perhaps how they respond to a spider in the bathroom too. Have you ever wondered why everyone is so scared of spiders but totally unperturbed by mushrooms? There are zero deadly spiders here in the UK, but a zillion deadly 'shrooms. So why aren't we all freaking out every time we see a shiitake in the supermarket? Why is fear of mushrooms pretty low on the list of recognized phobias? (It's called mycophobia if you fancy adopting it by the way.) The theory is that we *learn* most of our fears. The response is instinctive, but the triggers are often learned. So many fears are not in fact innate but acquired. I blame the parents!

Because I was a fearless child, I know my parents had to manage their own fears and anxieties rather than passing them on to me. My dad describes the stomach-churning fear he had when I came off a jump at a motocross race. I was going too fast and overshot the landing of the jump. To this day he describes how the image he had of pushing me around in a wheelchair lasted long after I had picked myself and my mangled bike up off the deck. Suffice to say, we stopped competitive motocross at this point.

*

Often our biggest fear is the thing we really want. It's the secret, innermost goal that we are too afraid to express in case we never reach it. I remember when someone from BBC Sport asked me if I was going to the Olympics and I thought, *I damn well hope so*, but I was too afraid of saying that in case I didn't make it and people would think I was a loser!

Similarly, during 2014 and the build-up to the Sochi Olympics, the thing I wanted most was to qualify after what had been one of the roughest winters of my life, with cancelled events and injuries chasing my tail. So, with just two weeks to go before the Games, the pressure was really on to deliver the best performance of my life, in a field of 40 girls, at the event I had turned my back on the year before. I did it, finished fifth, and I went to the Games.

A few weeks later, post-Olympics, I booked to take my motorbike test, and everyone was saying, 'Are you worried? Are you anxious?' But no, I wasn't bothered by nerves about the test at all, because I knew I could re-take it again and again and again (which, fortunately, I didn't need to). Competing in the Olympics is the chance of a lifetime. Doing your motorbike test? You can do it any time you want.

I realized that some opportunities only come around once. So you need to be fearless in approaching them and you need to put everything into them. Other opportunities, like driving tests, examinations, job interviews, first dates, making a soufflé – they're just part of the building blocks.

What's more, you must remember that they will never define you. However, there are different ways of preparing for different types of fear.

*

Back when I was starting out snowboarding, I remember being desperate to go to camp again. I'd hurt myself at Breckenridge in February 2007, so the fear was that I wouldn't make it to camp the following summer. I was desperate. We were due to leave America in August, but my parents took the plunge and supported me to go on to the camp in July before we came back to the UK. This time around, I found myself in the top group. Erin Comstock was the girls' coach; she was awesome, she was talented and she was sponsored by Roxy. I just thought that was the *coolest* thing ever.

I idolized Erin. I wanted to know how I could live a life like hers. I was always asking her questions. She was the person that I was looking for information from about how I could realize my goals. Until that point, I didn't know it was a possibility. Could I be a pro snowboarder? Could I be good enough? Would I be good enough? This is the thing I love to do and here is someone in front of me doing it. But my family are about to move back to the UK and they don't really have snowboarding there. How will I be able to do this? How am I going to make it work? The fear was really knowing *this is what I want*. I'd finally realized *this* was my sport.

Suddenly, everything felt impossible. I had to do my A-levels. There was no snow. There were certainly no mountains in Holywood, Northern Ireland. I was scared I'd never go snowboarding again, that I wouldn't have the opportunity to enjoy my passion.

Then, somehow, I started to chip away at the fear. I started undermining the fear. Attacking it with counter-arguments. I was constantly finding ways of reducing or shrinking the fear of going back to the UK and never snowboarding. I'd rationalize it. Shrink it down. Make it a non-threatening size. The mountains in Europe weren't far away. There's plenty of snow across the Channel. I was reassuring myself that there would still be opportunities for me to be able to do the thing that I loved.

I had started to build a vision of my future in the UK. I convinced myself that it was going to be okay, because I could use the opportunity to explore new territory. I realized that I could still snowboard. It would just be slightly different. I watched snowboarding videos and looked for places I could go. *There's Laax in Switzerland. I've seen lots of pros there.* By the time I'd finished turning the negatives into positives, I was excited to have a plan for what I would do when I returned to the UK. I was all set to get a job in a bakery or a supermarket. I'd save my money while I was at school and then go snowboarding in Europe. I was completely confident I could find ways to do it and enjoy it. I had managed to shrink the fear of not achieving my dream.

To be clear, at this point there was no expectation I was going to be a pro snowboarder. That idea was so far away and although I'd seen Erin and everything she did, for me it hadn't even taken shape other than as a teenage fantasy. It didn't even seem like an option, but I had begun to find ways in my mind where I could envisage snowboarding as a hobby when I moved back to the UK.

We left America and during my first week at my new school, Sullivan Upper School, I'd secured an interview by jokingly saying on the application form that I wanted to be a pro snowboarder. At that time it was just a joke and a distant dream, and I never believed it would be a possibility. But then, I came home to a phone call. Mum mentioned it was someone from Roxy and my first thought was *OH MY GOD!* I grabbed the phone: 'Hi Aimee, this is Stine Brun Kjeldaas from Roxy. I'm the Roxy European team manager and I want to invite you out to our Roxy Future Team camp next month in Switzerland. Erin Comstock recommended you to Roxy. She said you're interesting and she sent us your Sponsor-Me tape. We'd love to invite you out'.

Roxy is simply the epicentre of female boardsport, so to be associated with that, for me to get a call from them, was the ultimate recognition. It was everything I dreamed of and yet never imagined was going to happen. Here I was, being invited to join the Roxy Future Team, the world's best up-and-coming snowboarders. I had to go to this camp. I had to have a crack at this.

This time, I didn't miss the plane. When I got to the camp, I described myself as intermediate to advanced and listed some of the tricks I could do. Under the watchful eye of Lesley McKenna, a two-time Olympian herself, I spent six days on one particular jump, more determined than ever to learn. I might not have been the best, but I was willing to put in more work and hike back up more times than anybody else. I was putting in the practice. I remember getting my Backside 360 Mute Grab on lock, and securing my first feature in a magazine, *Document*. The feature was called 'Contender'.

After injuring myself on that rail at Breckenridge during that family holiday, I kept things simple on the rails and instead focused on the jumps. I was used to being in the air from trampolining in gymnastics, learning the backflip with my best friend, aged eight. Plus, I had a wealth of aerial experience reading lines and transitions on the track from the motocross years. I wasn't worried about the jumps so I hammered them and I felt fearless on them. I'd broken my collarbone on a rail, but I wasn't going to keep off the board. So I set about building my confidence in other areas, building confidence by repetition and keeping the thing that hurt me at arm's length. In essence, I had learnt to compartmentalize my fear.

I completed the Roxy Future Team camp in October 2007 and after that, Roxy offered to sponsor me. I couldn't believe it when they first gave me a jacket. And it was free! I had just moved back to the UK, afraid I was never going to snowboard again, and here I was being sponsored by Roxy. I was no longer an outsider. I was part of it all.

3

THE RULES – ONE STEP
AT A TIME

It's probably about now that I should spell out a few truths, some of the guides that have helped me reach my goals. These have evolved from the training and practice I put in. They have also been honed by the experiences I have had when dealing with challenges, which often involved dealing with a large amount of fear. While I'm not personally into the idea of 'rules', fear is one area where I use a set of rules (or concepts, or ideas, or pointers . . . don't feel obliged to call them rules).

Snowboarders would never be so uncool as to name them, but I do – between you and me – call them 'the rules'. That is exactly what they are. Hold them front and centre of your mind when you are doing anything, especially something that might leave you feeling out of your comfort zone, or in fact, any time fear raises its head.

Commit them to memory. If that doesn't work, write them on a Post-It note and stick them on your bathroom mirror, your fridge door, your forehead. Whatever. Just learn them.

Rule 1. Take it easy, be gentle on yourself and just do your best.

Rule 2. Any time you try something new, break it down to one step at a time.

Rule 3. Your nature is the result of every single action you've ever taken in the whole of your life. Accept it.

Rule 4. Everything you do has an impact on who you are and how you feel. Allow it.

Rule 5. It's normal to be fearful of something that you haven't done, so get used to it.

Rule 6. You have to expose yourself to fear and accept your vulnerability in order to grow.

Rule 7. Fear is normal so, if you really are afraid of something, just *do it* and see what happens.

This is the starting point any time you want to raise your game, learn a new skill or step up a rung on the ladder of excellence. So, how do you make that big scary speech or job interview or business meeting more approachable? Turning up in your lucky knickers, crossing your fingers and thinking you can busk it might work, but I wouldn't suggest it as a plan for long-term success. It's also no way to deal with anxiety or fear. The key is to prepare for the fear by exposing yourself to vulnerability in a safe way. It's about practice. And it's about perspective. The two Ps.

In terms of perspective, when I'm preparing for a major challenge, I look at the bigger picture. I zoom out to look at how simple my actions can be. To put everything into perspective, I make myself smaller than I am. In my mind, I almost shrink inside the big picture of what I want to achieve and look at what will drive me towards what I want. That might sound far out, but it's simple. Within each goal there are individual points along the timeline, and each individual point is filled with a number of mini hurdles to clear before you reach the goal. So the next thing I do is step away from the bigger picture and study the hurdles. Clearly, there are lots of small hurdles – an overwhelming number when viewed as a whole – but once you clear one hurdle, it takes you into a more positive space than you were in at the beginning.

You have to ask yourself: what are the consequences of jumping over that first hurdle? In other words, become aware of chipping away at the block. Each hurdle you jump, every time you take another chip, brings you a little bit closer to your goal. The trick is to put yourself in the moment and focus on how this one hurdle defines a part of your journey – the result is just one part of the bigger picture. When you are at the bottom of the mountain, the snow-capped peak looks like it's a long way away. It is big. You are small. But zoom out. Imagine you can shrink the situation by coming up to a bird's eye view of it. Scale everything out, sit on the periphery, look in, and you realize in the grand scheme of things how important the different elements are to you.

Making a situation smaller in the world brings your anxiety level down. Remember that everyone is fighting a different battle. At the end of the day, I'm the same as anybody else going through something. It's about keeping it in perspective. Then, look at the stages of the journey you need to go on to get to the end goal.

This is where you need to start breaking things down into a series of steps, the smaller the better. Once something is a step – an easy one at that – you can use that as motivation. The idea is that by focusing on breaking it down today, by enduring this feeling of difficulty (or fear), you know that you are one step closer to the goal than before you started. That's why you need to break it down into a single step.

It might feel like there are a series of life-defining moments, through which we rise or fall, win or lose. But there really isn't one defining moment. The reality is that there are lots of tiny but quite distinct steps. There are many, many defining moments in your journey and it is these experiences that create the growth that takes you to where you want to be.

No one told me this. I learned it through my career, by understanding that every single time I practised my craft, it was a moment that I could build upon. And it's that experience that often helps to carry you to where you want to be. This is so important. There's no particular defining moment. Each moment in the realm of what you do can take you a step closer; it's about consistency. Which brings me to the second 'P'. Practice. The more you do something, the more normal it becomes.

Think about the first time you drove a car: you're thinking hands at ten to two, clutch, find first gear, accelerator, handbrake, foot on the pedal. The first time you drive a car, it's a process so alien that you have to narrate it out loud. The more you do that process, the more you repeat something, the more accessible it becomes. So, the more time you have driving on the road and the more experience you have, the more you don't have to think about it. It's no longer thought. It just happens. It becomes automatic and that's how you become a better driver. It's the same principle with reading and the same principle with public speaking. Anything, in fact. The more you practise, the more approachable it becomes. It becomes normal.

I'm a great believer in standing in front of the mirror practising the speech that I've got to give, whether it's in front of five people or five hundred. I go into my bedroom, I close the door, I look in the mirror and I do it. The first time I do it, it's going to be embarrassing. Unnatural. Awkward. Plain weird. I know. I don't like doing it and it's embarrassing talking to yourself. But if I find it embarrassing talking to myself, how can I ever hope to stand in front of anyone else and talk to them? It's about learning how to be comfortable with myself in my own environment first.

Whether you're 18 years old and you've got to do a speech

because you're leaving school, or you're 25 and you have to stand up in the workplace, or you're 35 and you have to give a speech at a wedding, the trick is to get comfortable beforehand. You can't expect to stand up and just do it unless you've actually done it before. You have to expose yourself, in the first instance, to yourself. Then you can actually get used to the idea that you're going to make mistakes. You will mess up. Get over it.

Most people think they are either good at things or not good at things. People think, *I can't do that. I don't have the skills. I'm not a natural.* What's particularly interesting is that, quite often, people make that judgement having never even tried something! You want to know the truth? No one is born perfect at something. Every single thing takes practice. Athletes don't come fully formed out of an athlete factory. Contrary to popular opinion, they are not born that way. They are made. Or more accurately, they make themselves, through a series of life experiences and decisions, and practice. *Lots* of it.

Now, there might be personality traits or personal interests that mean you pick something up when you are growing up. If you end up as a famous actor, the chances are you were the kid who was dancing in front of your

31

mirror and you picked up an ability to do that and feel no shame. Subconsciously, you've been practising elements of your craft since you were a child. It happens organically. One of my teammates on the Team GB Olympic Snowboarding Team was called Billy Morgan. Billy came from an acrobatic background. I always used to wonder how Billy could get away with not going to the gym and not doing weights. He'd just rock up and be really good. Then it hit me. He was *always* practising. Not just on the slopes. Certainly not in the gym. It was just what he did. If he was in the living room, just watching telly, he'd be stretching. Or he'd be doing handstands outside the coffee shop. While everyone else was sitting on a chair, he was consistently practising his craft. He was doing it all the time! I realized practice doesn't always have to be done in a specific way or environment. You can practise wherever and whenever you want.

Obviously, there are moments in life that we're not passionate about but still have to get through. Times when we're not joyously dancing in front of the metaphorical mirror but we just have to get on with it. Getting to a place where we might be comfortable or we might find things more approachable is what's life about. The truth is, nothing ever comes easy. But there is a way to break down these obstacles to make them approachable.

No one's born with an innate skill to speak in front of 500 people. Nor are people born with a spontaneous ability to throw themselves down a mountain on a piece of carbon fibre. I certainly wasn't. So how do we get through those difficult moments in life that aren't driven by pure passion? That's where practice comes in. The best skills are learned subconsciously and consistently, and they all build up to define your character. It's a bit like cooking. Anyone can go to a cookery class and still make a terrible meal. But if you cook every day and taste what you make, and get feedback from the people you're making food for, then I guarantee you'll become a pretty good chef. It's the tiny, intricate details that people forget about or neglect to notice that drive you towards the bigger picture. All of these tiny steps have a big effect. They are all part of the larger picture and a lot of the time you won't even notice it. It's subconscious.

When it comes to skill acquisition, you can't say a trick is in your bag of skills until you can land it 100 out of 100 times. But you can't expect that until you've done it a certain number of times. For me, there are two different types of learning: learning by watching and taking on information from others, and learning by practising. Learning by watching can utilitze a huge range of media: reading and listening to books or podcasts, as well as observing others at work. I used to watch a lot of snowboarding videos, because you can learn so much from watching people. But the skills have to be physically learned and practised, too, so it's important to remember that the two types work together in tandem. There are no shortcuts or hacks. Repetition is key.

Take the front flip. I remember this vividly, because it's a relatively simple snowboard skill, but it's different to how you do a front flip on a trampoline. The difference is that on a snowboard you're moving forwards and standing sideways, so it's more like a side flip. On a trampoline, you start facing forward and land in the same position that you took off from. So the aerodynamics of doing it are different, but still transferrable *as long as you know how*. At first I couldn't do it because, every time I did, I rotated my body 90 degrees, and I'd land like I was landing on a trampoline.

It was frustrating. I could front flip on a trampoline. I remember learning how to do it in my garden. I remember the girls next door saying they saw me there at six o'clock in the evening and then they saw me there about nine thirty before they went to bed and then they saw me again at seven o'clock in the morning when they woke up. Over a 24-hour period, every time they looked out of their window, I was on the trampoline. Back then, I clearly remember trying to do a front flip. It didn't work. I kept doing it and doing it and doing it. Then, suddenly, I landed on my feet and it was like a light-bulb moment. It was like a nip and tuck in gymnastics – with a slightly faster tuck. I kept doing it. I thought it was fantastic. *I taught myself this. I've done it.*

Then, fast-forward to my snowboarding career. Eight years later, and I was in Laax, Switzerland with my coach. I thought *I can't do this front flip* and my coach said, 'Why don't I just show it to you?' He took his snowboard off and he physically did the motions with his feet on the ramp: weight on the back foot, springboard onto the front, carry yourself up and forward. Then he actually did it on the board. I copied it and I got it right. It was that one little action. One tiny detail. I kept doing it and from that moment on it's one of those things. It's in the bag. Once I could do it, once I'd learned the skill in that environment, I had to repeat it a certain number of times. The only way to learn a skill – to properly acquire it – is through repetition. To be truly accomplished, you also have to repeat the action in totally different environments.

Once I had cracked the secret, I could do the front flip, but the secret was a visual one. I had to see it, and I couldn't truly see it until it had been visually broken down for me. Once I could visually break it down and see the individual steps, I could put it back together. Then I had to do it, and feel it, and take that feeling. Like I said, a skill is never fully learned, but it can be practised so that it becomes portable and can be adapted to any environment. That's when you can take your speech away from the bedroom mirror. Maybe you've never done it for real, but you've done it before, for yourself. It's no longer alien territory. You've conquered the fear of the unknown.

I already had an understanding of this through my past experience in gymnastics and motocross. Both had helped me develop and demonstrate the discipline you need to do anything well. Ultimately, it was about two things – turning up and training. I only did gymnastics for two years, but I learned what it was like to train for three nights a week. Friday was conditioning night and I hated every part of it. Conditioning in gymnastics at age 10 to 12 was about getting some plastic ankle weights from Argos and doing a heap of exercise drills. It was about building strength and resilience, and all of that complemented the bigger picture of our gymnastics performance and enabled us to be better, but at the time I hated it. I did it because I knew it was part of the process, to get to where I had to go.

I wouldn't say I realized how important and valuable me going through those motions was at the age of ten, but it definitely helped me later in my snowboarding career. It helped me understand the importance of practice and repetition. It wasn't enjoyable, it was totally boring, but I understood that it was something I had to do. And this is not about tiger mums or pushy parents. Even a kid can understand, if you want to do x then you need to do y. It's like brushing your teeth. Nobody wants to do it, but you understand it's important. So you do it.

Every great journey starts with a single step. If you're stepping out of your comfort zone, preparing for something fearful or learning a new skill, always remember the two Ps: perspective and practice. Zoom in to see the tiny hurdles you need to overcome and zoom out to see the bigger picture you want to achieve. Then practise, practise, practise, because no one is born great at anything.

4

WHEN IN DOUBT, GO FOR THE BACKFLIP

I dreamed of being a professional snowboarder and wanted it so much but I didn't imagine it could be a possibility. However, when we came back to the UK and I got further into the school year, I began to see the opportunity. I wasn't afraid. In a Careers class I said, 'I want to be a snowboarder'. The adviser just laughed at me, saying, 'You can't do that as a job, you have to go to university'. My response was, 'I think I can' and from then on, I stopped going to Careers. I didn't need somebody to tell me I couldn't do something. I thought, *If I want to go to university, I'll go later, but I need to do this now*. It doesn't get easier when you get older. In fact, if I'd been two years *younger* it would have been easier.

I knew I might not be quite as good as everyone else – I hadn't grown up in the mountains or spent my life snowboarding – but I had this realization that with a bit of practice, I was in with a chance. I also brought with me the skills I'd learned in gymnastics, motocross and other sports, which is how the backflip ended up becoming my safety trick – I'd been bouncing for as long as I could remember. My friend Jaylan and I spent for ever learning how to do a backflip, hurling ourselves backwards again and again, so that by the time we turned up at gymnastics we were badgering the coach to let us do it.

When I first saw a backflip in snowboarding, I was like, 'Woah!' I *so* wanted to do it. I had mentally rehearsed backflips many times in my head and learned the skill in France. We built a little jump out of powder snow off the piste. You went down the run and came off this little poppy jump into deep snow, so you didn't have to flip very much. I just wanted the opportunity to do it and it was perfect. It could not have been a better jump – a small friendly jump – and because of that, my mental rehearsal and the confidence to do it, I landed it first time.

I remember riding at the British Championships, in March 2008 in Laax, and I can vividly remember me in this purple jacket and green baggy pants. I just kept on going round and round on this little lift outside of the competition because I wanted to do it again and again and again to make it better. But how do you rehearse something you've never done? I just did it in my head. A lot of times. And any time there was an opportunity to do backflips, I was doing them. On the trampoline at home, I'd strap a skateboard deck onto my feet with duct tape. So when I got to Laax I believed I could do the backflip because I'd done it on the trampoline with a skateboard taped onto my feet. I jumped up a few times to get the height, then I tucked my knees in, pulled them into my chest and kept pulling myself around until I was the right way up.

The backflip is actually a basic trick, but it is scary because you have to turn upside-down. If you go wrong, you land on your head. Not a good outcome. In fact, there are a fair few snowboarders on the world stage who would never even attempt a backflip. It's not for everyone, but it was something that was quite accessible for me and I was never really scared of it. So, what many other riders found frightening or risky I felt fairly relaxed about. I remember clearly thinking at the time that I could use that particular skill to make me stand out on the slopes. I definitely used it as a hook to propel myself in my career. I wasn't as good at spinning. I *can* spin, but I'm not as comfortable as I am upside-down. The backflip became my go-to trick if the jump was really big and I didn't want to do a spin. To be brutally honest, it was the trick that I could pull out of the bag if I couldn't do anything else on the jump.

However, focusing on the backflip probably wasn't the best step for my career because it distracted me from spinning flat, which gets harder later on. But it did mean that I could accelerate my career and earn money out of snowboarding. The backflip was the thing I could do anywhere, any time. It helped me stand out and it got me some serious magazine press, which led to sponsorship. It turned heads, got good photos in magazines and got sick video shots – and all of those things added together to raise the platform for my entry into professional snowboarding.

I didn't really come from a background where my mum and dad could fund my snowboarding, nor did I want that, so I think that's why I thought outside the box. For me, it was about needing to get to a point where I was self-sufficient. Now, I realize that I actually missed quite a few of the basic steps during my first few years of riding, but I know that if I hadn't made the call to pursue the head-turning tricks, I would not have been in a situation where I could turn pro relatively quickly.

I didn't realize as an eight-year-old playing on my trampoline that I was gearing myself up for my signature trick. I've mentioned already that we learn a lot from our fears – like when I first injured myself on that family holiday in Breckenridge – but we also spend our lives learning strengths too, and they can help us circumvent our fears. The backflip is something that naturally terrifies a lot of people, but because I had been doing versions of it since I was a small child, it was one of my favourite things to do. The backflip was my comfort zone – a strength that was very personal to me and my experience, that not everyone had. I guarantee we all have our versions of the backflip to help us through sticky situations and I see no shame whatsoever in making the most of them.

It is so easy to compare yourself to other people, especially when they can do something that you can't. But you have to remember that they've had thousands of experiences that have made them who they are and taught them their unique set of strengths. The thing to focus on is: so have you. I guarantee they don't have all the strengths you have, and they might be thinking the same thing about you. When you're afraid of trying something new or feeling like you're not 'enough', your own personal backflip can remind you that while you might not be great at everything (yet), you do have strengths that other people don't.

So, what's your backflip? What's the thing that you can do comfortably that might not come naturally to other people? Maybe you're an introvert, scared of confrontation, but you're a really good listener. When you find yourself in a difficult conversation and you're too overwhelmed to speak up, don't feel bad for starting in your comfort zone and leading with your strength. Listening is something we could all do more and it's surprisingly difficult.

The trick is not to get complacent. If all I ever did was the backflip, it would have lost its 'wow' factor and, to be honest, I would have been pretty bored of it myself. I tried to find a balance between learning new skills and practising the moves that scared me, turning to the backflip when I'd reached my limit. It isn't an exact science, and I was far from perfect, but knowing I had this one special trick really helped me reach my goals.

When your pulse starts racing and the pressure is mounting, your backflip can be really handy, but it's important that it isn't your only answer. You need a range of tricks to deal with whatever life throws at you. So, when fear strikes, take a deep breath and try to move slowly towards the edge of your comfort zone, safe in the knowledge that if it all becomes too much, you can always do that backflip.

5

RITUALS AND VISUALIZING SUCCESS

My first professional competition. I'm hanging out with the people I've looked up to for ages, people like Torah Bright, Jenny Jones, Cheryl Maas. I'm about to take part in the same competition as all my idols. What I had dreamed of and thought impossible when I was younger was actually happening.

Of course they were better than me, but it didn't matter. It just inspired me. I was excited to learn from watching them, because I could relate to what they were doing, and it was amazing. Assessing their moves, I knew it would take a lot of development to get to their level, but it gave me something to aim for and I felt for the first time, unlike in Careers, I could see the path before me. I thought, if these girls can do this, if they have already done it, why can't I? It was a classic instance of looking up to your idols and letting them set the standard.

Being at the Chicken Jam with my heroes also gave me a sense that this life was accessible. Part of me thought it would take more to get into the inner circle of this elite snowboarding world, but being there and seeing them at breakfast and in the van suddenly made it relatable.

I'd been invited to become part of the club. The opportunity was there for me to become one of their peers. Sure, I was looking up to them. But I saw no obstacle to being like them. They were just normal human beings. They were just like me and meeting them made my goal become more imaginable. With a strong work ethic, I was sure that I could sit at their table. It made me realize that normalizing a situation creates a sense of possibility. It's like, imagine if Usain Bolt lived down your street. If you saw him get up every morning and go to the running track, you would know he lived like a normal guy. He gets up, has his breakfast and goes to work. Remember, athletes aren't born, they are made. In fact, it's the same for any role or position in life. Your heroes are just like you.

Part of me worried, *Am I good enough?* But then I stepped back and thought, *Well, no pressure, I'm just the new kid on the block. Why don't I just kick back, have some fun and have a go on these big jumps?*

I had no idea what the open environment conditions at the Chicken Jam meant. When the light is flat you can't see very well, and it really affects your depth perception. Back then, I didn't really know how this could impact my performance. It was a little bit windy as well, which is a real catalyst for failure because it's dangerous and unpredictable. Of course, I was unaware of any of this stuff because – that's right – I had absolutely no experience at all.

If you rock up and do something for the first time, you have no idea how exposed you are to potential danger, so I was fearless towards this changing environment. Everyone who had more experience was much more tentative – *shit it's windy, fuck it's snowing.* I was just like, *I'm here with the girls. I'm part of this. I'm living the dream. I'm riding with Torah Bright and Jenny Jones. I've just been in the sauna next to so and so. Oh my God, they're ripped! This is what athletes look like . . .* The whole thing was such a learning curve.

Then, on competition day, everything came together:

a backside 360 tail grab. It was only really the third time I had tried this trick; I went at a bit of an angle and my hand grabbed the board. It was like awareness came to me, *oh, it's there, don't panic, it feels good, it feels right*, and it was. I grabbed the back of my snowboard, pulled it in and around…stomped it like a machine. Like clockwork. I ended up in the finals of my first ever professional competition. It was mad. I just got it right. I thought, *Holy shit, you're in the finals, where the hell did that come from?* But also, *This is where I'm meant to be. I'm home and I fricking love it.*

There's always some fear at the back of your mind saying, *I hope I do this, I hope I make it*. In the spur of the moment and the adrenaline of competition, that fear is eradicated. It's the same when you're running a marathon or riding a motorbike. In any event, there are underlying nerves, but if those nerves don't tip over a certain scale and overwhelm you, they are the fuel to your fire and allow you to perform at your best.

The Chicken Jam was my first competition and a World Stage event, so you can imagine my nerves and the potential to be overwhelmed. Visualization was key for me, especially as I hadn't snowboarded since November. I'd sit in Geography class at school and I would be visualizing the tricks and the things I could do. I didn't have that time on the snow but I had the ability to mentally map and visualize what I wanted. All I knew was that I was incredibly passionate about my sport and I really wanted to get better at it.

*

The night before any competition, I had a ritual. Just before going to sleep, I would stand at the window, whatever shape or size, and open it. If there was a balcony, I'd stand outside. I'd close my eyes, take a big deep breath. Then I would do the run in my head. Three times. I would take everything into account: the look, the feel and even the temperature. (Snow temperature can change over the course and affect your speed; cooler snow is much faster than snow that's even a few degrees warmer.) If I could do the run in my head, I knew I was going to be okay. And if I couldn't do it, I'd stand there a bit longer until I could put it together. Then I would sleep in my competition bib. In fact, I can still remember some of the sequences.

For me, this ritual is all about visualizing exactly what I'm going to do. It's my way of instilling a routine into my preparation. It gives me a platform of stability, knowing that I've done everything I can to be prepared. I'm taking the reins to control a tiny percentage of what is a very fluid and open sport. In snowboarding, as in most life experiences, you always have to be able to adapt. If you've prepared the basis for a scenario, you can then build on it or adjust it. By setting a precedent for the level I want to perform at, I know that I've got the basis to go out there and not just be okay, but to adapt by adding or subtracting a manoeuvre based on the conditions on the day.

Fog, snow, temperature, wind: there are so many variables. Wind is the worst. If it's windy, it's dangerous. You have to be ready to take it down a notch. Mentally, you've got to be prepared to do that, so that you're not disappointed or freaked out. You just can't get attached to a run that you've rehearsed to perfection. I know that I have to be okay on the mountain, so I can add to or subtract from the routine in any given environment. For me that preparation ritual of visualizing the course is about imposing some sort of base security. I can always tweak it on the day.

Then it becomes about peeling back a layer or adding one. Moving a block out or adding a couple more on top and that's about reading the conditions and responding to the environment. In competitive snowboarding you get two runs, but only one counts. The ideal situation is that you land your first run and you use it as an opportunity to build on and perform at a higher level for your second. You've got something good in the bag so you can only make it better. The security of a good first jump helps mitigate the fact that snowboarding is a sport with very little predictability. Play ping pong and you're in a sterile environment with no wind. You can rehearse your muscle memory to fractions of a second, perfect your backhand until you're a machine. But snowboarding is like sailing, it is totally influenced by the elements: the wind speed, the temperature and all the other atmospheric conditions. Wind, snow and fog can all take the speed off as well as impact your visual ability to perform.

When it snows, you lose all perception of depth, space and distance and you end up really dizzy. It's like vertigo. Snowboarders call it the white room. When the fog comes and the clouds engulf you, we call it socked in: the wind blows in the cloud, it's quiet, like someone's put a sock over everything!

Then you've got temperature. When it's -36 degrees, you

can't feel your fingers or toes. There's nothing you can do. Absolutely nothing. You can use heat warmers all you like, but your extremities are so exposed and when you've got to stand still for 20 minutes, you're numb with cold. Maybe you go up to a café for five minutes, but then you've got to drop in cold. So, what's worse? Being frozen like a block of ice and not being able to move, or being unprepped? For me, being a bit warm and unprepped would be a fair trade. Adapting to things I couldn't control and just had to deal with helped me to perform in any situation.

On a perfect day, with perfect weather, soft snow and warm sunshine, you can guarantee that everyone is going to deliver their best performance on the course. On a bad-weather day, you do not want to dwell on the what if: *What if it had been sunny? I could have done this. I wanted to come here and do that.* On a bad-weather day, there's a 95 per cent chance no one will do their best trick and, if you do, you're literally riding on thin ice. Like I said, it's about adapting to new environments and taking that experience with you. In the end, that became my biggest strength during that intense period of time: surviving bad conditions. It's simply about acceptance. You take a shit situation and you own it.

So, what are the skills I drew upon to ride the bad-weather days? First of all, I want to share the secret hack I developed: observation. Always take time to assess the situation. Don't dive in too quickly and don't be too quick to quit. It works before, during and after any given situation. Don't rush. Observe. This simple truth works on every level; assess before you make a choice. Look before you leap.

For example, I might be heavier or lighter than the competitor who's just fallen over on the first jump, so I take stock. I sit back, to see what everyone else is doing. I'll take a look at the girl who's riding the best; see how she's coping. Mentally, I imitate her state of mind and her movements. Mirroring. If she can do it, I can do it.

If you have the ability and the time to build each layer and then fix them together, you will end up with a stronger performance. I visualize it one block at a time. I build it from the bottom up and put it all together. It's about breaking your challenge down into a series of achievable events and then fixing them back together. I imagine the full run. But to get to the full run, I have got to break it down first. I use each practice session to conquer individual aspects and then put them all together. Each step doesn't just conquer the challenge, it erases the fear.

Up a mountain, there are so many things you can't control. That's why I developed visualizations and rituals. Visualization plays such an important role. It allows me to be prepared mentally for any eventuality.

Visualization became my pre-competition ritual. I used to start by imagining I was at the top of the run. Then, I jumped from the top to the bottom, successfully. I would go back up to the top and put all the pieces in place to make it to the bottom again, successfully. I used to visualize the jump, imagine landing it and anticipate the feeling of success. This was crucial. So, I would imagine I was standing at the top of the mountain. I would be strapped in and ready to drop in. Then, I jumped to the bottom and would imagine my smile and the feeling of accomplishment I'd get. Imagining that feeling of success is crucial. I would go back to the top and slowly work my way through the course. I slowed everything down to think about every single, intimate movement that I had to do on the course. I would drop in and then literally go through the turns that I would have to take to be set up on each feature.

*

Now, there were times when I needed to prepare and there were times when I had to make sure I didn't over-prepare. You've always got to go with instinct. My mum always told me to listen to myself and no one else (when it came to snowboarding, anyway!) – to follow my own instinct and ignore external pressure. The snowboarding environment can be incredibly volatile. Every single thing I did was intensely focused for a determined reason. I was always aware that if I made one false move, my dreams would be over.

I would always aim to get through 70 per cent of my run in practice, but there's an extra 30 per cent I would hold back to add when I felt the pressure and adrenaline on the day. Some boarders don't even do their tricks in practice. That's not my way of doing it, but I'd say 10 per cent of the whole field don't put their run together before the actual competition. But for me, prep was always key. So, let's say I've done my 70 per cent practice. I'm confident. It's the day before the competition. As I said, the night before, I visualize the whole thing. From start to finish, in my mind. Each feature is like a little puzzle piece and I put them together in my mind. In the build-up, while I'm falling asleep, I re-enact the visualization of the whole puzzle. I actually feel the pressure in the turns of each jump in my mind. It's my homework, subconscious practice that I do when I'm preparing to perform. So that when I'm on the slopes, I don't even realize I'm thinking. First, I break down each individual part of the competition route, then I break those parts down to get to the finish line.

*

This focus on the elements that build up towards getting to the finish line doesn't just apply to snowboarding, and I use it with lots of other activities in my life. Right now, my motivation to get up and out of bed that little bit earlier is that I know I'm carving out that time to nurture myself through physical movement, whether it's yoga, running or a workout at the gym. I love that feeling when I know I'm doing something for myself at the start of the day, owning that time rather than letting it be disrupted by life's noise.

I could never do a workout in the evening. By 6.30pm I'm done. I just want to chill. There's no right or wrong time to move, it's about what works for you and what serves your body and, most importantly, your mind. But for me, I know I will get the best version of myself if I get up and do it first thing. So as I wake up I'm imagining the feeling I'll have after a workout and that's what motivates me. It's very basic. I don't do it because it's good for me. I don't do it because I should do it or because I have to. I do it because of the feeling that I'm going to have afterwards. Once you've imagined that feeling at the end of a workout, you take yourself back to the beginning. Now work out. The day can control you otherwise.

Sometimes I don't even set a pace or a distance for a run. All too often that can be an added pressure, an obstacle to really healthy, happy, fear-free training. At the start of any journey through difficulty, I start by looking at the puzzle. I break the puzzle down into the pieces. There's no race to get there first. It's about the principle of committing to something and doing it. Sometimes, I'll go out for a run and I picture myself smiling at the end, 400 metres away from my door. When I'm not competing, when there's no real demand to do a particular amount or to perform at a particular level, one of my hacks is to set myself a slightly smaller goal than normal and then challenge myself to go further. Pushing further than I thought I was going to go. For me, there's no better feeling.

Let's take a walk. I think, *I'm going to go for a walk, make a couple of phone calls.* In my head, I deliberately don't set a distance or time limit. The fact that I don't set a distance and I don't set a goal means that when I make it back and realize I've walked five miles, I'm really chuffed.

What I'm saying is, don't obsess or fixate on goals. Be flexible with your goals and work around them. I don't beat myself up when I walk less. I think, I did five miles yesterday so today I'll do four miles. Accept that there are days when you're going to wake up and you don't feel great, you don't feel like getting up and pushing yourself. Instead of disregarding those feelings, cut yourself some slack. Lower the expectation. Nine times out of ten, you'll end up finding you exceed it.

6

SHIT HAPPENS FOR A REASON

I was with the GB Freestyle Team. We were all staying in a massive house and I really felt part of something. It was the start of the day and we all went to Keystone. We were having fun, all dropping in, making a train (which is where you drop in quick succession, following one another for speed). I was riding with a group of people who I considered my peers. A year earlier, they'd been my idols and they each probably had a decade of experience more than me. Basically, I was trying to keep up with a group of people who all had a lot more experience and my ignorance meant that I was unaware of what could go wrong. Learning how to judge speed is one of the basics of snowboarding. Too slow and you don't make the jump; too fast and you explode on the landing. But ignorance is bliss, although when it goes wrong you can really land on your arse. Literally.

We were riding along, four metres apart from each other, going like skittles off the jumps. There were three or four jumps in a row, so the person at the front set the pace and you had to hope and trust that they had the right speed. I knew I wasn't as good as some of the other girls, so I went last. I'd never ridden jumps quite like this before. The jumps were small, steep and very, very poppy. I went off the first one with total flappy arms – literally winding down the windows – and then I went straight into the second jump. I hit the knuckle, so I thought, *I'd better get low and send it in to pick up some speed*. All of a sudden, I was catapulted up in the air. Like, I really caught an air chair. My feet were no longer beneath me, but straight in front, as though I was sat in a car with the windows down. This is not how it was meant to be. *Shit*, I'd gone too far, I'd totally overshot the landing. I landed on the flat and felt like I'd impaled myself.

I remember the feeling vividly and I can only describe it as feeling like you've suddenly got a tail. (It also felt like there was poo in my pants, like something was moving in my glutes.) I rolled around on the floor with my stomach churning and then I thought, *Actually, I'm okay.* I sort of picked myself up and rode down very, very slowly. It felt like I'd split my arse. In fact, I'd broken my coccyx. I was told to sit around on a rubber ring for the next few weeks. I had this inflatable ring like a giant child's toy that I was supposed to use, but it was so painful I couldn't sit on it and instead I had to lie on my chest for a week. It's quite remarkable to think that bone is constructed from a flexible substance and it's amazing that the body knows how to fix itself and heal. But boy, did it hurt!

Now, I could have seen this as a massive setback in my snowboarding career, but I'm a firm believer that everything happens for a reason and this was no different. When I broke my coccyx, it felt like it was the universe's way of saying, *Yo buck, slow down!* The break in my arse bone was a kick in the pants for me trying a trick that I wasn't ready for. It was literally a brake on me going too fast. There are certain hurdles that I would have to go through to progress and this was just part of the process. It takes time. I will forever be the person that tries to run before I can walk, but this injury reminded me there's a process, which involves repetition, determination and willingness to learn. It was also a really good reminder that

I was not invincible. There was something Lesley McKenna once said that had scared me at the time. It was something I'd tried to block and suppress, but had now come home to roost. She said, 'You're going to get hurt in snowboarding. It's not a matter of "if" but "when", and you just have to be able to deal with that.' It made me realize, *Okay this is really quite painful*, but I didn't know how dangerous it could be.

After the accident, I tried to block out the sense of imminent danger and I managed to forget about it quite quickly, although I was left with a real fear of falling on my bum. While that injury left me with an instantaneous fear of getting back on the snow and feeling tender, I also really understood how it went wrong. I knew that I would fall on my arse again. But I would never fall on my arse to that degree again, because I could understand where I made an error of judgement: I went too fast and I let the jump buck me like a donkey.

Another reason for shit happening is to prompt you to reflect. Success is easy; it's failing that's hard. You have to find the positive in all outcomes. I had to ask myself, *What is the positive outcome of this break?* Well, the positive outcome was that I realized I was going too fast and needed to slow down. I also needed some qualifications *just in case* and it gave me the opportunity to lie on my belly and do my coursework for the A-levels I was meant to be studying for.

I apply this logic to all aspects of my life. What good can I take from this accident or setback? It's a trick I learned from my mum; she always searches for a reason why something happens to comfort and console you. If you can find the positive in a negative, you create your own support by giving yourself permission to be okay with something. So, something good really does come from something bad. I ended up getting an A in my PE A-level and that was only because I applied myself to the coursework. More than that, though, I learned that I had the ability to apply myself to things that are important to me. The specific learning from this was: judge your speed or you will get hurt. The bonus is that I got the top grade in my PE A-level. So, breaking your arse can be a good thing. Sometimes.

7

KEEPING AN EYE ON
THE REAL PRIZE

By December 2011 and into the 2012 snowboarding season, I was absolutely loving it. *This is my life! This is the shit! My dream has come true!* I was officially a pro snowboarder, competing internationally as a sponsored athlete. Snowboarding brands were now paying me to do what I loved. I'd signed a three-year deal with Roxy and my position in the sport was looking somewhat more secure. Discussions with energy-drink sponsors lay ahead, so things were going well.

But the Olympics wasn't even a proposition for me back then. I was just living in the moment and loving it. I vividly remember buying my mum and dad flights as a Christmas gift. That feeling of being able to give something back to them was great. They came out to the newly named Roxy Pro in February 2012, in Saalbach Hinterglemm, Austria.

It was probably the first event where they saw me well and truly thrive on the world stage. I was in my element. I came third, next to Cheryl Maas and Jamie Anderson. Did it feel good to have my parents witnessing my success and having us live that journey together? Boy, did it! I was on fire.

I knew I was in a good position. I was fresh off a 2011–12 season-opener win at O'Neill Pleasure Jam and secured my third place at Roxy Pro with Mum and Dad looking on, but I didn't allow that to consume me. I was just focusing every time I was on the snow, making sure I got as much practice in as possible. I was robotic. I was on autopilot. I was in that complete flow state. My batteries would just be constantly charged. Fully stoked. *Let's go!* Let's get this right. There was precision, there was focus. I put everything into it and that showed in my riding. Those were some of the most vivid moments of my life.

Opening that season at the 2011 O'Neill Pleasure Jam, I was so in the zone. The guy on the mic was loud, but I couldn't hear him. Everything was like clockwork. Tick-tock. Tick-tock. Bish-bosh. Bish-bosh. Bash. Attacking the course every single time. Landing, landing, landing. I had spins three ways. I had the cab underflip – taking off switch landing regular – and the back seven – two full rotations. Then, I would charge towards the last hump, back rodeo with backside spin, I'd look for the landing, stomping it switch with my back foot forwards – and finally I heard the guy on the mic shout . . . 'she's riding switch!' I wasn't even resorting to my safety run. Everything worked. I loved it and I won.

I had an expectation in the back of my mind that I would kill it that day. I wanted to land on my first international 5* podium. I knew I could do it, because I was keenly aware of the standard and the level at the competition. I just felt good. I felt like I was on fire and I was ripping. A podium spot was mine for the taking. The only thing that could divert me from that goal was if I was distracted by my environment or by other people, but when I was riding, I was like a robot. I barely spoke to anyone. I just went for it.

I had a friend called Rupo and he rode beside me. He was like, 'You've got this, it's yours,' and I loved having someone there that I trusted and who supported me as a friend. He kept saying, 'You're on it, you're so there, just put it together when it counts.' The way I did that was by continually replaying what I wanted to do in the practice. I wasn't scared of losing, but I was hungry. I'd tasted success and I wanted more.

Looking back, I think what kept me hungry was the fear of going back to normal life and attending university instead of snowboarding. I just didn't want to do that. I'd had enough of school. I knew what I wanted. My real fear was not being good enough and returning to being a casual snowboarder. I didn't want to be a casual snowboarder. I wanted to be a *pro* snowboarder and I wanted to be able to do it whenever I wanted. I wanted *that* life. I'd seen it in America. I'd seen the lifestyle that competitive snowboarders had and that was what I wanted. The only fear I had was not being at the standard that I wanted to be at. So I put the graft in. On those windy, icy days when I just wanted to go back to bed, I would get up and do something. Because I knew that something was always better than nothing.

To manage the fear of not being good enough, I invested the time on the gym floor, making my body robust, and I invested in the snow time to progress my learning of the sport I loved. I had set a clear goal. I'm not special, but I thought that others have done it so why can't I? I just had to follow my passion and respect my body. I believed that if I focused on my snowboarding and my riding ability, then everything else would fall into place. There was lots of learning to be done, but I knew that if I turned up and did my best, all the other elements would come together.

I had discovered that living my dream was a possibility. I'd never thought it was possible, so there was a definite realization that this doesn't happen to many people. I knew some girls that were ahead of me had an easier route into the sport, but I believed that if you really want something and you really work at it, it will come to be. It's about manifesting the future you want.

I could have been distracted by the idea of going to university. That might have diverted me from my goal, but I thought *I've only got one shot at this*, so I just had to do it.

I realized that you can always come to school later in life – you can go back and do exams – but there are some opportunities that only come round once in a lifetime. So, I had to take a leap into the unknown. I had to put all my passion and energy into that. I knew that my greatest fear was to end up in a place where I was thinking, *what if?*

I knew I didn't want to live in a state of wondering what might have been. I knew that it was the right decision to follow my dreams. If I had waited, I might never have made my career as a snowboarder and I would have lived in a perpetual state of *what if?* I knew enough to understand that golden opportunities aren't always there and sometimes they are just to do with timing. If that time comes along and you don't direct your energy towards your goal, you might miss that window of opportunity. I made the decision to put my heart and soul into what I loved doing and have a career as a professional snowboarder. That was the 'if'. And if I hadn't put my energy into it at that precise moment, I can pretty much guarantee I would not have made it as a pro snowboarder. I would have been a bit older. I might not have got the same sponsors.

Life is sometimes like being in a boat on a river. Imagine you're in a river taxi. There are two stops: the stop on the right-hand side is university and the one on the left-hand side is snowboarding. I figured that the option to study and go to uni would always be there, but the opportunity to become a professional athlete and dedicate my life to the sport I love, and ride for a brand that pioneers female boardsports, would only come along once. I knew that if I chose not to get off at a certain stop, I might live my life wondering what could have been at that stop. You see, the stop on the left was a temporary stop. If I didn't get off, it might not have been there the next time I rode that river.

The stars wouldn't have aligned. I would be sitting here today thinking I wonder *what if* I had made the decision to go full time?

Now, I have to make a confession. I did actually try that stop on the other side of the river. In 2009, I had ended up at university, because there were fantastic resources and, if nothing else, I thought I could use their facilities. I messaged them with my A-levels and I got into Bath University. I didn't really know what I was signing myself up for. I went for a couple of days, introduced myself and was like, 'Hi guys, nice to meet you, cool, this sounds great,' and then I was like, 'I'm sorry, I've got to go now, I'll see you next year.' I hadn't sorted a full term's accommodation, because I had no intention of actually staying. I ended up doing the first semester online.

Meanwhile, in the snowboarding world there was a hype in the air about me. It felt really good: I was riding well in 2009–10 and the British board test was at the end of the season in Austria. I remember having some really good days riding well, feeling very confident on the board. I was now full time on the GB Freestyle Team and they knew who I was. I was just ripping. Turning heads. I never went out for drinks at that time. I was staying in doing my coursework, hurrying to get it finished. On one of the last days of the board test I thought, *Why am I doing this?* I really wanted to be a snowboarder and university wasn't going to help me. I can really recall that moment, being at the board test and everyone going out for drinks, while I tried to finish my coursework, knowing that I was really turning heads and my career was taking off. I just knew at that moment that I would be doing the right thing to focus on snowboarding. So, I asked if I could defer my university course. I ended up deferring for the next three years, just because I was in the zone. Apparently, my name stayed on the register for the duration of that course. They used to joke, 'I wonder if Aimee's coming?'

At that stage of my life, I was living so much in the moment, with such presence. I didn't want to have any regrets. It was 2009, the year that I officially went professional, meaning that I could make a living from the sport – contracts were secured and my board, clothing and footwear were assigned to brands. It was a total transformation from winging my way to events and making it happen (including sleeping on airport floors), to now riding with the big guns and having an eye on the UK Sport funding purse. All my mates were at uni accruing debt (there's nothing wrong with that, but it wasn't for me). I remember paying for my first year of university with the money I earned from snowboarding (my careers teacher would never have predicted that)! I only went to uni for two days, but I can say I passed one semester. I just knew I wasn't going back to study.

Looking back, was I fearless? No, I wasn't. But at that time my dream was coming true and it all started to feel like it was becoming possible. There was no fear in turning my back on university because I could finally see there was a path to my dream – I just had to ride the rollercoaster. I couldn't have one leg in the UK at university and one on the snow because that just wouldn't work for me.

Elements of the journey were not the way I imagined, but I used them to my advantage. I might have been one of the shortest riders on the snow, but I realized I'm also one of the strongest, so if I did hit that knuckle I'd ride through it and the rest would fall over. It was about finding my own path and owning it; it was time to hedge my bets on professional snowboarding.

I was finding my physical strengths as well as my inner strengths, and capitalizing on them. I'm small and I'm strong. I might not be the heaviest, but I've got stronger legs. I found the things I could believe in, so that when the situation arose and I needed to find that inner strength, I could go, *Yes! My lifeline is strong, hold on*! I was actually pre-programming strengths I might need so that, in a moment of fear, I would know they were there. Reassuring myself that I had these strengths in store for whenever I might need to use them.

At the root of it all, whenever I've really doubted myself, I know I can reach out for external support. My family has always been there for me. My mum and my dad have always said, 'Yes! Go for it! What's the worst that can happen?' My support network is vital.

Make sure you're always around good people. As my best mates and I say, 'energy creates energy'. I look for good energy and use it as a morale boost to continue the drive for whatever I'm aiming for. Then, I go back in my mind and recall past experiences, so I can use them as a platform to take things one step further. I use this technique to remind myself that I've been here before, it's felt like this before and I've succeeded before. That kind of knowledge builds confidence. Use the positive feelings from those past experiences and build on them. Remember them. Then, use them as a platform for growth.

8

THE FLOW STATE

You can run the same route 365 days a year, but the minute you give it a label, stick a number on your vest and put a finishing post on that run, you change it into a competition. You can guarantee that everyone is going to run a different race. In the lead up to a competition, there's a series of steps on the way to mastering a trick. Or any skill for that matter. You over-practise the range where you're comfortable, so it becomes so accessible, so easy, that you know it's just sitting in your back pocket. Then there's a deep focus point and it might take you a while to get there. For some, it might take you landing your first run in an event to reach that new level. Let's assume you're following the rules and you've done the best you can do on that run. The next option is to run off the adrenaline and step up again.

Progression and skill acquisition can happen in all sorts

of different environments. I was always fuelled by the pressure of an event, that gave me a stimulus. It gave me that little bit of an extra nudge. For me, the thought of winning an event is a spur and an inspiration. Adrenaline can really raise your game, as well as help to manage your fear.

Approaching any goal, there's always a sense of fear. In my case, there's often a fear of injury too. It goes without saying that serious injury is one of the greatest risks in snowboarding. Which means that one of the biggest challenges is finding the point where your fear of injury meets your fear of being under-prepared. How do you reconcile the risk of knocking yourself out of the competition through injury with the fear of not being prepared? It's a really fine balance.

You've got to be in the right space mentally and physically to respect your ultimate goal. To get close to that, you have to look at the simple building blocks of your goal and break them down. Then, deep practice is going to take you to a place where you can do this task in the automatic part of your brain. It's what I call cruise control.

It's not easy to achieve. First, you need to get rid of the fear of injury by practising intensely at the level that you feel comfortable with. As usual, there are different levels of practice. One level is so practised, it's automatic. This is when the skill doesn't take conscious brain power. Like cruise control, you can't really say that it's you consciously doing it. Once you're comfortable in that range of cruise control, then the next step up means there's a lot less room for anything to go wrong. The cruise control is so fluid that it's almost in danger of becoming boring, which brings us to the next stage. This is the bit that has the extra ingredient: excitement.

To take the cruise-control metaphor further, you only ever want to try to change gear when you're comfortable at the speed you are cruising at. So, once cruise control is your new normal, it's time to step up a gear. You raise the bar, you start to acclimatize again and soon get used to cruising in that new gear.

Being in flow state is different: you're hyper aware of what you're doing, you're totally present. Everything comes together. You're no longer standing on your snowboard, it's a part of you and it moves with you. You keep going and going and going, almost until someone tells you to stop. All the cogs are turning and moving in the right direction. It's the same feeling as when you put the pieces of a puzzle together. You pick up the piece and you drop it in exactly the right place.

Flow state is like tunnel vision, where the only thing you are conscious of is whatever it is you're doing. The only thing you see is what's ahead of you and everything else is just white noise, a distraction. In flow state, you're so tuned in and focused on what you're doing that there could be someone playing a trumpet one metre away and you wouldn't even notice it, because you're that locked in. Flow state is when you are in that zone.

It's not an easy place to get to, and when you mentally achieve that state you don't necessarily think, *Great, I'm here!* In fact, you're so present that everything just flows. One move goes into the next. There are no distractions. It's just you and the task in hand. You can't hear any noise, other than your own thoughts. I first became really aware of it in motocross, but I didn't know what it was. Then I became hyper aware of it at my second Pleasure Jam win, in 2012. I wasn't aware of it during the race because I was so focused, but it was as if everything ran like clockwork. Even the wind wasn't a distraction. I was like a machine.

I remember at the Pleasure Jam, there was a snowboarder on one of the other teams. She was a girl who you never wanted to be sitting next to on the lift, because she was like a race deterrent. She came up to me one day saying, 'Aimee, it's so windy,' and I had to be stone-cold focused and ignore her. Later, people were coming up to me and saying, 'Aimee, you're riding like a machine!' I was in such a fluid state. I didn't feel fatigue or fear because I was so present in what I was doing. It was like, *This feeling is so great. I just want to keep doing it.*

Back in the motocross days too, I would be so focused on the experience, so focused on myself and in the moment, that there were no distractions. That was when I started to feel the rhythm and the emotions of the track. I started to know where each bump and nodule were, and I started to know the feeling when you hit the first peak at the initial table-top. When you land smoothly and the tyres touch the ground. You open the throttle, lean over, bank to the left, next corner . . . It's when all of that becomes automatic and you don't have to think about it. It just flows and it's like a rhythmic movement.

In the early phases of learning, the actual actions aren't fluid. They are quite lumpy. But the more rehearsed and practised they are, the more fluid they become. There's less mental processing. It just sails. There are no bumps in the way; no mental blocks that you have to overcome. You just flow through each part of the process. There's a guy on the circuit called Henry Jackson who has the loudest voice ever on the mic doing the in-stadium announcing. I know if I can hear Henry, then I'm not in the zone. When I stand at the top before I drop in, I'm closing my eyes thinking, *Take me to the place where I can't hear him.* If I can hear Henry, I know it's not the one.

People often ask athletes, 'Hey, did you hear that roar from the crowd?' But when you're in that moment, it's like you're surrounded by cotton wool. It's just muffled, distant background noise. The only things you can hear are your own thoughts. Your body is directing all of your brain power to the senses you need, so hearing doesn't matter. Sometimes you don't even necessarily need to see. Flow state focuses all of your brain power on only the parts that are essential for you to perform. It's a feeling of being as one with the board, with the bike, with the road, or even on the footpath when walking.

*

These days, the most in the zone that I become is when I'm doing yoga. Yoga's probably something that I would have thought wasn't cool or was too slow when I was younger, but I've discovered that it's a really challenging way to channel your focus. It's something so simple, yet it's so hard not to be distracted by outside voices. It's the one thing that kept me sane through the two Olympic cycles of 2014 and 2018, and in 2016–17, when I was on the whole international-travel hamster wheel doing six different events back-to-back across continents. Yoga was the thing that kept my body and my mind together.

My routine is yoga. But my yoga routine doesn't stay the same. It's not a particular style. I don't really have a set of moves. If you had to name it, you could call my routine movement. Because I'm always on the go, being able to adapt is vital, so I use what I have around me to perform some sort of movement. This sets me up for my day. I have a routine, irrespective of where I am, but the practice *is* the routine. It's about finding this, doing something regularly that can be fluid depending on what job you do and what your specific needs are. It's different for everyone.

For me, yoga is something with absolutely no pressure. I never want it to become something that's about performance or progression. It's really just about nurturing my body. Some days I'll do a little more, some days a little less, but yoga is never something I want to push or get better at. Certainly not with my previously broken wrist, which makes my yoga repertoire somewhat limited. In terms of my schedule and fitting in the things that serve me, they have to be flexible. Each day follows a flow from waking up through to igniting. I'll start the day with some lemon water. Then some coffee (a lot of coffee). Then I'll get into something that's going to make me sweat or release some tension, whether it's yoga or a gym session. My routine is informed by my environment, which is ever-changing depending on what I'm doing. That's the only way that I can commit to a routine, by giving it the flexibility to move with me.

Between 2014 and 2018, yoga saved me. I did yoga every morning before I snowboarded and every evening after I'd snowboarded. The pace of life as a snowboarder was hectic – swapping time zones and adapting to different courses all around the world. So yoga became my comfort blanket, a way of finding some sort of stability while living out of a suitcase in a hotel or an apartment or a flat with a teammate. It's portable. You take it with you and you slot it in anywhere, in any space. When you've got six contests back-to-back each week in different countries, how can you have a routine? When you're changing time zones it's hard to be diligent about sticking to certain times for a workout. You can really screw yourself up. Our theory was always to maximise sleep rather than fighting the jet lag. Then there are logistical issues, like finding a gym that's open. You have to be flexible. Do half an hour in the morning and half an hour after riding.

What's great is that sometimes if I needed an extra 15 minutes sleep I'd still do yoga, but I'd be flexible about it. I'd do 15 minutes in the morning and then do 45 in the afternoon. I could commit a certain amount of time to yoga, but it still allowed me to be super-flexible in terms of when I did it. It wasn't about any equipment. It wasn't about a gym. It was a commitment to a mental practice and a physical practice that gave me the confidence to know that I'd done everything I could to prepare the ground for what I was trying to achieve.

I travelled with a yoga mat. You can do it with a towel, but travelling with the mat meant I could lay the mat down on the ground at night so when I rolled out of bed, I'd be on it. Or I'd lay it out in the kitchen so when I woke up (and was thinking of bailing), I was standing on it with a coffee. The physical act of having what you're doing laid out the night before for me is a big one. Even now. For example, last night I knew I was going to get up early to go for a hike, so I laid out my shorts, my socks and my shoes. When I got up in the morning, there was no question about what I was going to do. That simple act is a big part of my commitment. It's stating an intention, then following through.

In a work capacity, stating an intention and following through is my commitment to what I'm doing. It's non-negotiable. It means my mind is at rest. I can't forget. I'm not fumbling around searching for what I'm doing and I'm not able to make any excuses. I'm making the commitment the night before to achieve the goal that's going to take place in the morning.

In terms of my kit – if I have decided to go running the next day – I lay it out on the floor. When I wake up, there is no choice about what I'm going to wear. I've committed to the action, because I'm going to run. In the winter, if it's cold, I put my trainers, socks and all my clothes on the radiator and then there's really no backing out. When I put the stuff on I'm roasted, so I need to get outside!

The hack is to remove the obstacles in front of the task. For me, the yoga mat is a call to arms. I've put the mat down the night before. It's waiting for me. I can't get out of bed without walking over it, so I can't ignore what I'd planned to do. It's so simple, but it has literally changed my life. Trust me, it works. You don't believe me? Do it tonight.

It's not *I should*. It's not even *I could*. It's *I can*. I *can* go for a run, because my stuff is there. I *can* do yoga, because the mat's already out. I *can* have a great day at work, because I prepped my bag the night before. I'm visualizing myself doing the task.

In 2019, I ran a marathon in North Korea. One of the things I thought was *I am so blessed to have a body that can transport me over this distance*. I thought that was amazing. Just the ability to run. To walk. There are so many people who have disabilities, injuries, missing limbs. Whatever your physical situation, be grateful for what you have. That's what I was telling myself. I'd never run a marathon. I'd never even trained to run a marathon. In those moments, when shit is tough and a simple thing like putting one foot in front of the other feels hard, see if you can put that into perspective. Realize you're fucking lucky to be able to run. Look after what you've been given and use it because it is a gift and it's a gift that not everybody has. Look after it. Respect it. Use it well.

9

HOW TO GO FROM
'YOLO' TO 'OH NO'

I was the first woman to do a double in competition, and it was a huge progression in my snowboarding. I was one of the first people to ever land this. It was, officially, a landmark moment. Just to unpack the double, it's a double backflip – two somersaults, to be precise – in the air, halfway up a mountain.

The first time I did the double was in New Zealand in the summer of 2012. I was chasing the tail of progression and, to be honest, I simply saw it as a step to move my career forwards. I liked being upside-down, and I figured it was something I could do that would raise my profile. I had just been signed by Red Bull. I remember driving my electric blue Mini Cooper out of Northern Ireland, across to Scotland on the ferry and down to London. I went into the Red Bull offices and picked up my freshly painted Red Bull helmet. This level of sponsorship had been a goal in my career. It was the pinnacle for me at the time.

Red Bull has an international all-star team. They look for young aspiring athletes who are going to be or already are the world's best. To be recognized in that light at the time was a massive deal for me. I had become a Red Bull athlete. There is only one person from each country who snowboards for Red Bull and being sponsored by them meant I had been recognized as one of the world's best.

One of the big parts of being a Red Bull athlete is having access to their training facilities. They were one of the first companies to come up with a reduced-risk training environment. They had airbags. They had trampolines. You were able to train, take risks and push the envelope safely. It was also exclusive. There is only a tight knit crew of people in the UK who have been given that seal of approval, who wear the Red Bull athletes' hat.

I'd been invited to the Red Bull pre-season camp in New Zealand, where they had their reduced-risk training environment. It looked like a bouncy castle and, given that I was so comfortable upside-down, I was just like, *Let me on it!* I wanted to see where I could take my body. It massively reduced the fear of injury while I practised the double. It was almost fun. You could still get hurt but, if you got it wrong, you weren't going to land on the ice – you got to land on a giant bouncy castle of air. Imagine doing a backflip on a bouncy castle, then multiply the speed of that by eight. If you land on your neck on the airbag it will still hurt, but you aren't going to be leaving the mountain in a wheelchair. It certainly took the sting out of it.

No joke – the Red Bull helmet gave me wings. I absolutely ripped the socks off the next three weeks on the mountain. I landed the first double I tried in New Zealand and it was all over the internet. AIMEE FULLER LANDS DOUBLE IN SNOW PARK, NEW ZEALAND. It was a headline. I knew it was going off, that this would be my time. Going there and landing the double, the emotion going through my head was sheer elation. I'd landed it in front of the right eyes and it was going to propel my career forward. I took it as a very positive step and moving into the first part of the 2013 season, I felt that I was unstoppable.

There was undoubtedly something about the magic Red Bull helmet that made me feel invincible. Clearly, there's something psychological here. At a superficial level, there was an element of looking good and feeling good about it.

That helmet was the seal of approval on the international circuit, but it was not just about endorsement or being in a club. There was a huge amount of support. I was the only female snowboarder from the UK in the Red Bull team. It was pretty special. It's like being accepted into an elite family of athletes. It was go time. Later down the line, however, it became an added pressure. In times of struggle the feeling changed.

So, why was landing the double turning heads and getting me noticed? Like the four-minute mile, it hadn't been done by a woman in competition before. Now it's nothing special, but at the time it was my mission to be the first woman to land it in contest. I wanted to make a mark and to have a world first. I wanted to put my name in the history books. It was a progression for women's snowboarding for sure. It was also a personal triumph and sense of achievement too. But looking back, I realize that I was so distracted by wanting to achieve it that I neglected training for my Olympic qualification, which is a big regret to this day. There's a deeper underlying story here, one that was going to cause me a huge amount of struggle and teach me a massive lesson in life.

I was pursuing the double with such ferocity that I had

completely forgotten about the Olympic qualifiers. I remember riding in the Hintertux Valley in Austria. I was doing doubles consistently and I was feeling really good. I won the Pleasure Jam in November and then headed out to the States for the first big contest of the season, which was the Dew Tour in December. Around that time was also the first big Olympic qualifying event, but I really wanted to make my mark in the Dew Tour, because that's where the X Games look when they want to choose their top eight girls.

The Dew Tour is this monster event on the snowboarding calendar in the States. It's one down from the X Games, which is the absolute pinnacle. Dew Tour is pretty showy; they've got television, lights, cameras and the big brands are interested because it's on television. The Olympic qualifiers, such as FIS World Cup events, are different. It's actually run by the Ski Federation, there's drug testing and it's all very down the line. The Dew Tour is about shiny moments, TV time and sponsorship. It's a massive, snowy, winter set for us to compete on. Just to be invited to be on the Dew Tour is a massive thing.

When I arrived, I was on a complete mission to do the double and get noticed by the X Games. I wanted to be the first woman to do it. I remember I pulled one in practice, stomped it and then it got to qualification. I rocked up. The double was on my mind and I dropped in. It's funny, because my nan always says that I must have drunk too much Red Bull. I felt jacked up. I dropped in, did a cab underflip on the first jump and then I sent it into the second jump. Fear was non-existent. I so wanted to land the double, I ripped it. But I ripped too hard, which meant I went round two-and-a-half times, smashed into my back and rammed my shoulder into a bank of snow. That was me out. I'd damaged my rotator cuff. I was done.

10

A CRISIS OF CONFIDENCE

After the accident, I had a grade-two tear in my rotator cuff in my shoulder. The first thought I had was, *Am I okay?* I guess the response was, *Yes and no.* I was in a lot of pain and I really couldn't use my arm. The chance of qualifying for the Sochi Olympics in 2014 was leaving the building. *This can't be happening; I am part of Team GB. I am on the road to the Olympics, en route to Sochi.* But I had a busted shoulder and worse than the pain was the fear of falling on it again.

In 2012, we lost Canadian freestyle skier Sarah Burke at the age of 29. She was one of the world's best half-pipe skiers and she was my friend. Sarah was a talented, beautiful, kind and generous person. It was devastating. Moments like that brought into perspective how dangerous snowsports are. There are few sports that operate at that level of danger. It scared me; it scared everyone. All I could think was, *I don't want to put my family through that.* I knew my sport was a mental strain on them. The roller-coaster of emotions that I put them through was savage. Dad would often say, 'When I saw that last jump I just thought, I don't want to push you round in a wheelchair for the rest of your life.' The fear was real.

I always knew that if you want to achieve something you can't just have it as a goal. You need to put the steps in place to achieve that goal. But in the lead up to my first Olympics, I was far too relaxed. Looking back, I realize that I had become complacent. I was totally fixated on landing the double on the world stage and my obsession with that deflected all my energy and focus away from the Olympics. It sounds arrogant, but I just believed I would be going to the Olympics. I had this simplistic, positive outlook that I would qualify. Little did I know, there were actually a huge number of obstacles. The injury I had incurred as a result of pursuing the double was about to become a massive learning opportunity. It didn't just cramp my style, it made me incredibly aware of falling. It made me feel something I'd never felt before – I was nervous. I was in pain. I was so worried. It hurt. I went from wanting to do well and land rad tricks, to full survival mode, which is not fun. This was the start of a long 18 months.

My physio Ali was getting me to creep my fingers up the wall when I realized, *This is going to take longer than a week*. The first Olympic qualifier for Sochi 2014 was coming up, just 10 days after Dew Tour. How could I fix this? The answer was, I couldn't. But I could still gain experience – and that is how, just three weeks later, I found myself at the top of a run with my arm taped to the side of my body, about to drop in. I was about to compete in the first Olympic qualifier – at the Copper World Cup in early January 2013. Slopestyle was a brand-new sport in the Olympics. I had never done an Olympic qualifier before.

The greatest fear I had was fear of injury. If I'm injured, I can't use my body and the minute I can't use my body, I am no longer a part of the process. You could say this was fear of the unknown or fear of the future, or even fear of pain. I guess it was really fear of missing out. Fear of injury manifests because, if you are out of the game, there's an enforced break. Sometimes that break can be beneficial – like when I broke my coccyx – but, depending on the timing and duration of the break, it can also be detrimental. An injury can make you hungry, but you can also get left behind. That's where fear creeps in.

Something is always better than nothing so, just by being at the qualifiers, I was gaining an awareness of what to expect when I was in the competition. I knew that anything more than just getting through the course with my arm taped to the side of my body would be a positive. I reframed my expectations.

So, the Olympic qualifier came round and I had a floppy arm. I was thinking, *It'll be fine. It has to be.* There are only a certain number of Olympic qualifying events and you even get points for just turning up. If you land in the top five, you get a load of points, so that can guarantee the elite riders go to the Olympics. I knew that I had the ability to ride the course to get a few points on the board and keep up the progression. My only goal was to get down the course. I knew I had the ability to go to the Olympics. So, I had to just rely on that.

Of course, no one wants to show up and just tick a box. I wanted to show up and make an impact. If you get first, you get a thousand points but even if you're forty-ninth, you still get a couple of points. I should know. I came forty-ninth. But even just by showing up and putting up with the pain, there was validity in going to the qualifiers. However, I would never get enough points by coming forty-ninth. I was demotivated at that point and I had very little understanding about how important each individual event really was.

The next event I took part in, just seven days later, was the 2013 World Championship in Québec, Canada. It was mid-January. Again, the jumps were big. It was -40 degrees every day. It was windy and icy. I was properly scared. I hated it. I was so scared of hurting myself. I didn't feel in a position where my body could take the impact. I was standing at the top and could see no way for me to safely, never mind successfully, ride the course. Slowly, but surely, the other riders made their way through the course and were coming back up. There was no single part of me that wanted to do this. I didn't want to get hurt again. So I decided not to do it.

I could hear my peers and coaches shouting, 'You can do it! You've got this! We'll work on this!' The more they kept on, the more I just looked at them in a vacant way, thinking, *I don't want to do this. I don't want to do it.* At the top of that slope, I made an appraisal based on my recent injury and continuing pain. I told myself, *Aimee, you have the ability to remove yourself from this situation. You have the ability to stop these feelings and leave this emotion.* I weighed up the potential disruption that further injury could have on my dream and I made a totally conscious decision not to compete. Walking away was a positive action, rather than a negative one.

There have been so many times when I have had to suck up the negatives because I know there'll be a greater positive outcome in the long run. But when I was standing at the top of that slope in Québec, all I could see were negatives. I was confident in my decision. I had bigger fish to fry. I would practise my skills so that, next time, I wouldn't feel like this. I was crystal clear. Mum always told me never to do anything I was uncomfortable with. 'We will never be mad. We will never judge you. Just do what you want to do and don't ever put yourself in a situation where you're uncomfortable.' I didn't feel up for it. I didn't feel good in my body. I didn't like the course, so I said no. I'm not doing it. Would any other top athlete do that? Probably not, but I knew in my heart that I didn't want to deal with the consequences of getting hurt again.

The decision was about finding the right level of discomfort in myself. Something had changed and I was not willing to enter a situation where I felt in danger of hurting myself. It was about managing my injury and understanding how injury can knock your confidence. I made the conscious decision that I was going to own this, take myself out of the environment and put myself somewhere where I could heal my injury and strengthen my weaknesses. I chose to take myself out of that hostile environment so that I could return fitter and go further. It was a hard decision to make at the time, because it meant missing a qualifying event. But I knew it was a necessary step for me to be able to come back stronger and be comfortable in that environment when it mattered most.

*

During this season my attitude had really changed. It went from this essentially old-school rock-star mentality – all about doing the double, getting it down, pushing my progression – to the feeling that my Olympic chances were being taken further and further away. Later that year, in Canada in July, I actually managed to take yet *another* hit and injured my acromioclavicular joint in my left shoulder. *Okay Aimee, that's not helpful.* The following month, I was in New Zealand for another World Cup. New Zealand is windy and icy, and the jumps are big. It's a bit of a survival game. I got through the course and only finished twenty-fifth. To qualify for the Olympics, I needed to be in the top 12 and there were only two qualifying events left. I'd come from the top, with progression, excitement, loads of big events, and I now was like, *Shit, I'm nowhere near going to the Olympics.*

There's no doubt that this season created a massive turning point for me and was filled with ups and downs. I had gone from feeling fearless to recognizing and respecting the part fear has in teaching me what is the right and wrong thing to do. I believe you can always take a positive from a negative. The pain, emotional impact and the damage to my confidence of my injuries had made me cautious and afraid. I was listening to that fear. At the same time, I was turning a negative into a positive in Québec by making the decision to leave and come back stronger.

Sometimes the most important thing is removing yourself from an environment and knowing what you need to do, physically and mentally, to be comfortable in your performance again. Put in the work elsewhere to excel next time.

*

In November 2013, I was due to go to the Ski Show. It was a big media day, the start of the Olympic season, and I remember telling my mum that I didn't want to go. 'There'll be tons of press asking me questions about the Olympics and I haven't qualified. I really don't want to go'. But she said, 'No, you should go. You're going to the Olympics, unless someone tells you otherwise.' That one phrase really stuck in my mind. *You're going to the Olympics unless someone tells you otherwise.* When she said that I was just like, *Yeah you're right, no one's told me I'm not going. So, I'm going to do it.* I went to the Ski Show feeling positive and when a journalist from the BBC asked, 'Are you looking forward to Sochi, your first Olympics, the first time Slopestyle is in the Olympics?' My response was 'Yeah, I am. I can't wait to represent my country on the world stage.'

You're going unless someone tells you otherwise. Those seven words shaped my mentality. I think my mum underestimates how much that one sentence inspired not just my motivation, but my destiny. It restored the belief in myself that I was going. There was no other option. I had to believe something that wasn't actually in place. I had to believe it was going to happen.

The Olympic qualifying process is quite deep and there are a lot of moments in there that defined me. Over a period of 18 months, the experience totally reshaped my approach to my career and to life in general. It set a pattern for me to have good time-keeping and to be accountable. Before, I was always a bit slapdash. I would just rock up and wing it, but those Olympic qualifiers were big, defining factors in my life that changed the way I do things now.

There are different types of pressure. Some are definitive and others are not definitive. For me, qualifying for the Olympics was the definitive pressure. It was something I really wanted and really cared about. When I later transferred that feeling to other opportunities, I had a greater ability to deal with pressure. It really taught me what was important and what wasn't. And if the outcome doesn't matter, then it won't define you.

11

FOCUS OVER FEAR

While the pressure of Olympic qualifiers and the fear of injury seemed to dominate my 2012–13 season, there were some moments of real highs where I was able to fully focus and achieve new feats in competition. In Tignes it was sunny and hot. That's my vibe. The double was the fifth feature of my run. I was so focused on landing it that I nearly forgot the other elements. But I knew I had to perform all the features successfully to achieve the goal. I was about to become the first woman to land the double in competition, but to get to the big goal I had to pull off every step along the way. That was the process.

When you do a double, you have to take off with momentum, so I didn't want to go too slow because

I'd come up short. But I didn't want to go too fast either, or I'd end up at the bottom of the landing like a dozen eggs dropped from a two-storey building. It's all about getting the speed right and the pop just so. So, I was riding in and I powered into it. I was coming in to take-off so I went through the ritual. I visualized the jump. I gave it 20 per cent more than during the practice. I exploded from the core. I went round and round again, and I was thinking, *great.* I stayed tight. I could see the landing. I touched down and it was heavy. I'd never really experienced landing that heavily in an event. There was almost twice the momentum that I was used to. Plus, I went a little bit further than I intended and in that brief moment one of my knuckles smashed into the floor. It was so quick you couldn't see it, but it was like getting your hand and smashing it into the ground ten times harder than you could physically punch it. I didn't know it at the time, but I had broken my finger. It hurt like hell but I was clinging on. There was still another feature to go. Done. Through the landing. Then there was one more rail and I was thinking, *don't mess it up, I've done it, but I have to hang on.* I cruised across the rail, super-easy, landed and felt utter relief. I had finally done it. I was the first woman to do the double in competition. No one else will be the first to do the double. That's always mine. And it felt cool.

But how did I know I was going to do it this time? What had allowed me to overcome the fear that I might fail? I visualized the tricks before I did them. I got them to work in my head before I tried them. I approached the course like it was a puzzle, figuring out which trick could go where. The next step was to take it to the course. Usually, you've got two days to prep before you actually have to compete. I used those two days to acclimatize my body and mind to the course. I worked through the feelings associated with the action, the speed and the physics that I needed to successfully negotiate each feature. Not many people break it down to the feeling, but for me it was more than just finding out the speed required. It was understanding the feeling of the speed underneath my feet and the pressure I was going to feel on each take-off. I then visualized it again and again. Step by step.

Imagine a bag of tricks. If you're always taking one of them in and out, that trick is more likely to be at the top of your bag and easy to grab when you need it. The tricks you have lurking at the bottom of the bag are more difficult to find, but you can make them more accessible by taking them out more often – you just have to practise reaching for them. By keeping the double near the top of my trick bag, through visualization and then practice, I made it easier to reach when it counted.

My environment on the day always feeds into how I feel and for me the environment at the X Games in Tignes was a good one. Mum and Dad were there; I was with my Roxy teammates. It felt like everything was on steroids: the lights, the banners, the TV. You actually feel like you're on a movie set and that environment just gave me the oomph I needed. I basically put everything into getting it done and the jumps were good; they were the right size, everything just clicked. It wasn't even a question of whether I should do the double. I was just there and I was going to do it. I realized that I had to not make it a big thing in my head. Sometimes you can analyse every single moment, break down every step. When there's too much analysis, things get tense. I had walked away in Québec because it didn't feel right. In Tignes it felt right. I knew I'd practised.

The best thing about it was that I was back vibing. I'd put in the work and I felt good. Unfortunately the next two Olympic qualifiers – in Russia and Spain – were cancelled due to the weather, so even though I was vibing, the competition environment wasn't vibing for me. I only had two qualifying events left in which I had to pull everything out of my trick bag – when it mattered most – under the most intense pressure: one in Colorado and the other back in Québec. Those two events would play a huge part in building who I am, what I am and how I approach what I do. My coach worked out what the minimum requirement for me to get into the Games would be. I needed to be in the top 12, or top eight or top six, depending on who else was in the running. I had two chances to crack it.

I rocked up to Copper in Colorado and I was just on a mission. I became this robotic machine. Eat. Sleep. Train. Repeat. I had an intensity and focus completely different to anything I had felt before. I had never applied myself to anything so seriously. I'd always been this free-spirited YOLO, let's do it, believe in yourself, live your dream kinda gal. I'd never had such a defined goal or regime. Now, it was: I get up, I eat, I train, I come down the mountain, I eat, I prepare and use recovery techniques in the gym, I eat and I go for a walk. That walk, half an hour every night – whatever the weather – that was my therapy session. I found peace and silence, capturing my thoughts and mentally rehearsing what I was going to do each day at the event. I remember December in Colorado was a howling blizzard, so I would put on some music and I would stroll. I would use that solitude and that time on my own to process my thoughts and work out the route to achieving what I wanted to happen on the mountain. I would trot along in the blizzard and work it out. It was my therapy, my visualization time and that was a big, big part of my routine. The weather was awful, but I didn't care. This was my opportunity to do what I do best. It didn't matter what the weather was doing. I was going to use it to my advantage. I knew if I practised robotically, I would have what I needed in my trick bag. I would be able to reach in and grab it when the time came. You can do everything to prepare, but you cannot overthink the process of an event. You rock up, you talk to your friends and when it's go time you just have to silence the noise and focus solely on what you are doing, and it just happened for me.

This was a different type of goal: a numbers goal. It was raw competitiveness and I was fighting for my place in the Olympics. This was not about the vibe of snowboarding. This was about beating my opponents and I had never been that person. Normally, I'm not competitive. But at that moment, I wanted to beat everyone. I needed to prove myself to the judges. I knew it was about me, what I could do and how I could use the environment to my advantage. It was snowing. It was windy. The jumps were slow, but I didn't give a damn. I had trained. Everyone was going down like skittles. I could see where the other girls were going wrong and I made the decision not to follow. There wasn't enough speed, I knew I was going to knuckle the jumps, but I wouldn't be falling over. I just decided that I was not going to sit down. There was no questioning my motive. I stuck to it and I landed my first run, which meant I needed a top 12 and a top six, depending on how the rest of the field performed. It held me at eleventh place the whole way through the contest. There were 60 or so girls. Everyone had two goes and my first run held throughout the whole event. I didn't drop out of the top 12.

But I couldn't get excited about it, yet. I needed two top 12s to hit the Team GB criteria and I needed to be in the top twenty-four in the world. The event in Copper lifted me up to about twenty-seventh in the world. I couldn't let this consume me, but it was a positive step in the right direction. I knew there was still work to be done. I had three weeks until the next event. The last Olympic qualifier. This event would be the one to decide whether I was going to live my dream. And it was in Québec.

Of course, the weather was shit, but my attitude was that I was going to own this. I knew I couldn't do my best tricks, the conditions wouldn't allow for that. So, I was going to be the best version of myself on the course and it would just have to do. It wasn't about being pretty; it was about survival. I remember landing my first run. I muscled my way through. There was so much snow on the ground, there was no speed. I remember tucking in, being strong and agressive, and pumping and pumping and literally just getting over the knuckle of the jump and touching down. Because there was so little speed, everyone was landing on the knuckle and falling over. I watched that throughout the practice and the qualification, so I was like, *Okay I'm going to knuckle* – which is hit the deck hard – *but I'll just suck it up and ride on. I'll do better than the other 64 girls.* And I did.

*

They never announce the Olympic team in snowboarding until after the last event, often just two weeks before the Games. And the reason they don't is because the scale of qualification is so flexible. It's all influenced by conditions on the day. Even the most closely controlled sports have moments influenced by the environment. For example, in the 100-metre sprint, if there's even a little bit of wind, Usain Bolt may run 0.001 of a second slower. When you're in a really open environment, competing over the course of three days, the weather plays a huge part in the outcome. That's the sport. Shifting your routine to fit an ever-changing environment and landscape.

I went to Québec with one intention. I was going to smash it. This was my time. Nothing was going to divert my mental game. I can still visualize the course in Québec. I knew what I had to do. I went there on a mission.

I vividly remember arriving in Québec. I had missed Christmas at home to get there on time, the first time in my life I hadn't gone home for Christmas. I'd flown to Toronto where my cousins live and spent Christmas there, because I wanted to be in the right time zone. I'd ridden the mountain near Toronto, which was one of the first places I had ever snowboarded, and then I went to Québec.

I was so in the zone; it was like I was going to war. I knew I needed a top six or better. If I fell, I wasn't going to the Olympics. I was on a mission and I was going to achieve it. I was keeping myself to myself. All the British team had decided to fly to Québec via Boston but I had thought, *It's January and we're going to stop somewhere that's famous for having the worst weather in North America.* Boston Airport's always closing. I had decided I was going to go my own route and I was going to go two days early, because I didn't want to risk turning up for my last chance to qualify and have my snowboarding bag turn up late, or be stuck in an airport lounge for 12 hours and miss practice. I was not going to allow any of this shit to go down right now. I didn't have time on my side for hiccups. So, I had taken myself down to Denver and I remember being at the airport five hours early because I didn't want the stress of anything going wrong. As predicted, the British snowboard team got stuck and lost their board bags and missed a day's training. By the time they arrived, I was already there, chilled, rested, with all my kit, and had done a full day of training. Inside, I felt like I was going to qualify, but I knew I still had a long way to go. There were 38 girls in the final competition. All 38 girls have two runs and their best run counts. Only five of us were going to make it through. This was intense.

*

I fell on the first run of the qualifying heat. If I didn't land the next run, I wasn't going to the Olympics. Just a *little* bit of pressure then. I headed back up to the top, thinking, *No, no, no, why did I let myself fall? I didn't come here for this. I have to put every single bit of experience into this one run, otherwise my dreams are over.* I couldn't let the pressure overwhelm me. I had to quickly push the negativity away and try to focus on the task in front of me. At the top, I started chatting to my friend Torah Bright, who is *amazing*. She was only there because she needed a few more points. She's this really happy-go-lucky, positive-energy kind of girl, and in true form she was up there dancing, or 'doing a boogie', as she calls it. I was like, *yes! This is the vibe, I'm going to get on this.* And we just started dancing. It was -40 degrees and we were frozen, but we felt positive. When I dropped in, I was singing. *This is just another run. I can do this. Don't overthink it. Boom, boom, boom, boom*, landed it, smashed it. *Yes! I've done it.* I was in the top 12 and into the semi-finals, where I needed top six. I had a whole day of waiting for the semis, which felt like for ever.

The next morning, I woke up and thought, *I have my trick bag. I've got my tricks. I know how to unpack them. I've got this.* I was the first one through the course and I charged through it. There was a bit of wind, a bit of snow, but it felt like nothing. This was all me. I was in my element. I practised my run. Dropped in for the semi-finals. Smashed it. Landed. I was standing sixth and no one could overtake me. I'd done it. I was in the finals and had another three runs to go, but they didn't matter. I considered not even doing them, because I didn't need to, but my coach said, 'Just drop in, you might surprise yourself'. I went along with it and it turns out he was right because I ended up finishing in fifth place instead! I was going to the Olympics! I qualified with just two weeks to go. It was a defining moment for me.

What's hilarious is, without me knowing, my nan and grandad had already booked flights to Russia! I didn't even know if I had qualified, and they had made their minds up. Two weeks later, I was on my way to the Sochi Olympics.

*

The mental turmoil of that process, of staying in a positive place, of holding my focus on the visualization – that level of concentration was the most intense thing I have ever done. It consumed me. Nothing else mattered. I can often get distracted by stuff: by work, by life, by being busy. It's easy to be distracted by outside goings on and before you know it, you've wasted a week because you've been distracted by outside voices. I realized then that if you really, really want something it's going to take an extreme level of concentration to get it.

It doesn't mean you won't enjoy it or you won't get pleasure out of it, but if you really, really want to do something – perhaps something that scares you – you just have to do it. The main thing that clicked for me during that time was my mum saying, 'You're going, unless someone tells you otherwise.'

Beyond the focus, discipline and training, what I really learned was self-belief. Not to limit myself by what I *think* is possible. Not to fear what I think isn't going to happen. Become your dream and don't let anyone tell you you're not living it.

I don't think I will ever experience pressure like that again. I felt the distance between me and my goal grow and grow until the very last minute and, even then, in that single defining run in the semi-final, if I had tripped up in the start gate or mistimed a jump, I wasn't going to the Olympics. It totally redefined my sense of fear. My greatest fear was not being at the Games. Sometimes we can get hung up on things happening a certain way and we bow to the pressure of perfection. I'm the first to admit that my first Olympic journey wasn't pretty, but in the end, it didn't matter how I got there. I was on my way.

12

CLIMBING THE LADDER

I can't lie, snowboarding isn't low on risk. I've had a lot of injuries in competition and in training. It's like anything else. If you don't practise it, you get a bit rusty. When you're competing, snowboarding should feel just like running. You just get up and do it. But, just like running, if you don't practise that's when things hurt more. The problem with injury and snowboarding is if you hurt yourself too much, you miss out on competing. But if you don't train hard enough, you're not going to be in the zone for competition. It's a fine balance.

Every destination, every journey, really does begin with one small step and every big achievement is the culmination of a series of very tiny steps. There are short-term goals and long-term goals and the way you create a ladder to them is by using short-term goals as the rungs to reach the bigger goals. Goals are vital. Everyone talks about setting them and reaching them – but for me their greatest importance is in terms of managing fear. I use goals, but I keep them flexible. I change them. All the time in fact.

Sounds wrong, doesn't it? But it works.

One of the biggest lessons I've learned is that a goal is not restrictive. Goals are not a fixed series of levels or steps. Instead, imagine them as a ladder. You can visualize the rungs as colours, as numbers, or even as a pyramid, but the point is that it's a scale. This ladder visual is one I often reach for when stepping out of my comfort zone to acquire new skills.

*

Lesley McKenna had been my coach for the Roxy Future Team and she taught me about the micro-steps on the ladder of excitement. Lesley is a three-time Olympian. She became Head of Team GB and was a Roxy Rider before becoming the Roxy Future Team manager. She was there throughout my whole career in some capacity and she was the one who showed me that success was possible, but only if I put in the graft.

As a result, I was never afraid to ask her for help. She's tiny, but so strong, mentally and physically she's a tank! And someone who showed it was possible. She had all the fundamentals to nurture talent, because she'd been to the Olympics herself. She was confident, calm and a fantastic mentor. If you watched me riding at my peak, I'd be cruising and being explosive, you'd be thinking: shit, what's going to happen? Lesley had that same explosiveness, and sometimes she would push it beyond that line of fear, something that I never did. She always had her own unique style, whether it was clothing or riding I'd always looked up to her and will call her a friend for life.

She helped me learn to manage fear by studying the building blocks to success. For example, take the fear of missing out. If your fear of missing out is because of a fear of injury, that's going to hamper your training big style. You really need to eradicate that fear, or you aren't going to train effectively. How are you going to train if you are too scared to try the thing you need to practise? So, you have to tackle the fear of being hurt first. You reduce the chance of hurting yourself by working out the building blocks in regular practice. The individual blocks need to work at a level where you can snowboard like you walk. The goal is to be so comfortable and to reach such a level of confidence that you have no fear of missing out, because you know you have done everything to protect yourself. You want to feel like you're walking down the mountain and you do it in gradual levels, starting at your comfort level.

I learned that you can't just go out and do it. It's all about risk assessment. There are patterns and steps in snowboarding that allow you to get to a particular trick in a safe place. Goal setting for me became about repetition and practice. Setting a specific target and then using micro-steps to get there.

*

My process of goal setting has evolved over time and a lot of it was about learning what I could become comfortable with, and pushing that to get to the next stage. I would visualize a mental map for dealing with fear, especially in terms of competition, when it really counts – the ladder of excitement. If you imagine the ladder as a series of ten comfort zones and at the top there is a circle: the circle of fear. The bottom of the circle is the beginning of where you're fearful and at the top is where you are really scared. So you want to be practising at level seven, which is the edge of that circle, and as you go up that ladder and you step into level eight, you start to become acclimatized and you can deal with the fear.

The ladder is a scale of progression to take you to the best level of performance in anything. It is a way to assess where you're at and it's a way to learn how adept you are at moving out of your comfort zone. So, on a normal day going about normal-day stuff you're essentially bopping around on the three and four levels. Moving up a gear is when you're starting to need a bit more focus on whatever it is that you are doing in order to perform well. Through six and seven you're looking at learning things you might not have done before, or aren't fully comfortable or practised in. I know when the pressure is on, when it's game day and when the crowds are watching, I can get to seven if I need to without too much prep. I might be fearful of it, but I've done it before and I can do it again. For me, that would be like the cab double (switch frontside 180 into a double backflip). Moving up a step to eight is where you know you can do something, your foundations are solid, but you're feeling the warmth and excitement of the fire and feeling the danger that comes from stepping out of your comfort zone. At this point you know that a bit more pressure will help to get you in the next zone. Just to be clear, it's not a ladder of fear. It's a method of managing and assessing progression.

It's about unlocking different levels to push to be the best version of yourself, so those goals will always evolve. I sometimes see it as a spice ladder to recognize what level of heat I'm at and what I need to do to move higher up the ladder. So I want to be able to operate reliably at seven. But the ladder is constantly recalibrating and as I practise, things move down the rungs as they become more accessible and operational. Frequency is the key to owning your progression within the ladder. There's no shying away from hard work, and let's be honest, that's what's required for any success.

To achieve higher levels of performance in anything, you need to be constantly climbing the ladder to unlock things. At the same time, it *is* okay to sit in the middle of the ladder and over-practise something until it's boring. The ladder helps me operate for an extended period of time at a certain level, while still looking ahead to progression. If you over-practise something until it

The Ladder in terms of Spice. What level of heat are you at?

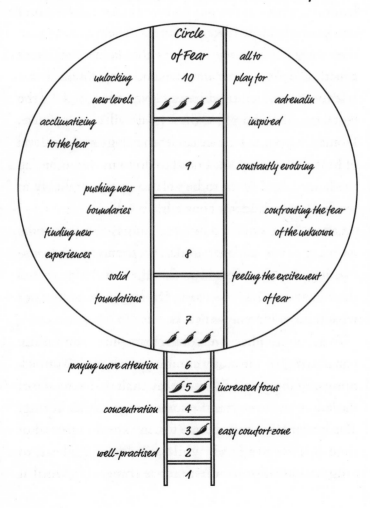

becomes easily accessible and so boring you're on autopilot, then you know you are ready to take the next step up the ladder of progression.

As someone who didn't live in the mountains, being constantly at level seven was so much harder for me than it was for other riders. I was rocking up riding at level five and then going straight into level nine. This was a pattern I found throughout my career. I've been to level nine and ten – and that's where you really feel the fear – but the whole principle of the ladder is that you acclimatize to the fear by practising at a lower level.

Often, I step back and imagine myself standing at the very top of the ladder. It looks dangerous but, because I've built the steps to get to the top and I've practised those manoeuvres, I feel safe. On top of the ladder, it's important to remember that I'm also in the warm circle of heat. So number ten, representing fire, can also be comforting in the way that fire can be too. There's a sense of danger and a sense of adrenalin. The heat lifts you up. It inspires you. You want to go there. It's just about mental attitude. Once you are comfortable up at the top, it's all to play for.

Each step brings you closer to your biggest and boldest

move. Potentially, there is danger ahead, but you make yourself safe because you've practised everything, so it doesn't feel like you're at the top of a ladder. You feel safe in the bubble of excitement.

13

WALKING WITH FEAR

Coming out of the Sochi Olympics, I remember feeling pretty positive. It had been an amazing experience. It was full on and I think what I took away from it was learning about different types of pressure. I came out of it with a smile on my face. I think the Olympics taught me about not pushing yourself beyond what you're capable of. I had learned that I had to do what suited me.

Afterwards, I wanted to get off piste and show people what I was capable of. So, I went on a trip with two friends to Silverton Mountain, Colorado. It's a 'free-ride mountain', the Mecca of back-country off-piste boarding. This free form of snowboarding is so good for the soul, taking you back to the elements on natural, off-piste terrain. When you are out there in the back country there is a real sense of adventure, of excitement and of taking it back to its roots. It's a blank canvas for creativity, where you spot features in the alpine terrain and ride them. I wanted to go out there and shoot some different, vibrant footage to show what I could do away from competitive snowboarding. I got most of the things I wanted to film. I had it done and then I listened to my gut instinct, which told me to go back home to spend time with my boyfriend and my family, which has always been very important to me.

At the start of April I went to the Red Bull camp. I arrived with fire in my boots. I was still riding high from the Olympics and went there to make a point, on a bit of a mission. This was the first time the cab double had even come into practice for me. There were only three or four girls who had done it and I wanted a piece of this puzzle. I was there to challenge myself. Even though I had made it to the Olympics, that wasn't the end of my journey. I decided I wanted to be up there among the best, so in a way I really had a point to prove. I was one of the best riders and my goal was to continue on that train of progression. I got to the camp and went into this robotic mode, where I just kept knocking it out. I remember landing 17 out of 19 cab double nines.

I learned how crucial mindset and resilience are when you want to achieve something. It all went well at camp, apart from damaging my thumb when I landed on my mate. It was one of the early practice days. There were tons of people on the jump and they were all shouting 'Drop!' They hadn't noticed that my friend Dara had actually fallen over in front of me, because at a certain ability you drop really quickly and at this level people don't really fall over. She was fine, but her skis came off and as I came off the jump, I could see Dara on the floor. I literally put the brakes on and missed her, but landed on her ski and rammed my thumb into it. I was so annoyed because I had hurt myself unnecessarily and it was pretty bad. I couldn't move my hand. So, for three days after that I was just cruising with my thumb in a brace because it was too painful to do anything. Once that injury subsided, I came back with even greater enthusiasm. I'd been sort of held back by my thumb, but I took a positive from what could have been a negative. The power of the thumb.

When greater powers tell you to slow down, I always believe it's for a reason. I realized the thumb just made me hungrier and made me observe the process of what I wanted to do more. Because of the thumb, I took a step back. I watched everyone else. I re-visualized the process and, when the pain died down and the brace came off, it was like lighting the blue touchpaper on the rocket. I was off. I was learning that an injury can be positive. I was learning that a break in repetition or practice is an opportunity to recalibrate and reimagine success.

I've always had the ability to see the positive in a negative, and I suppose that is a gift. But it's also been something I've developed and worked on. That is definitely a lesson I want to share with people. I can pick seven things at random that I'm grateful for – my mum, my dad, my brother, my grandparents, my friends, my house, my health. But it's so easy to have a negative spin on things. I know people who might say I've got a house, but it's in the wrong area. Some people search for negatives in everything. You could say, 'Oh my God! Putney High Street is rammed' or you could say, 'Isn't it great? There's a real energy in Putney High Street'. This is deeper than spin. It's bigger than denial. It's about seeing what the thumb can teach you and being grateful for it.

To be clear. It's not just a mental trick. It's not about a stiff upper lip or looking on the bright side. Though that helps. Sometimes you do just have to overcome a failure. Sometimes you do just have to tell yourself it's not all bad and it could be so much worse. I mean, I didn't break my arm.

*

However, there comes a point every now and again when an injury is so bad and so out of the blue that no amount of learning from it can set you straight. On 31 December 2016, just ahead of the biggest year of qualifiers in my life, I sustained a grade-two tear of the lateral ligament in my ankle. That winter had started in Milan. My qualifying season had got off to a good start and my sole focus was qualifying as soon as possible and not leaving it to the last two qualifiers as I did in 2013–14.

I wasn't even snowboarding when I got injured. I went on a walk with my boyfriend of the time down Slieve Donard, one of the biggest peaks in Northern Ireland. I hadn't even been interested in going but we wanted a bit of time alone, away from everyone. The ground was uneven, typical mountain terrain, and I stood on a large branch, hidden beneath leaves in the woodland, and aggressively rolled my ankle at force. It cracked and I thought I'd broken it so my boyfriend had to carry me the last mile-and-a-half down to the car park. I have a gammy ankle and have struggled with my feet before. I was so scared that it was going to affect my ability to achieve my Olympic goal. *Why me, why now of all times?* Just when I needed to be in impeccable shape and form – mentally and physically – to achieve what I wanted. It made me want it even more. I was so frustrated. I was meant to be flying to Russia the next day for the first Slopestyle qualifier for the 2018 Olympics and I was like, *Why has this happened?*

This was the first time ever in my life when I actually thought, *Why me, why now, what have I done to deserve this?* I was experiencing self-pity. This was new and it was annoying and frustrating. It just sucked. That was my instant thought response. My knee-jerk reaction. But I didn't really have time to wallow in self-pity. Maybe that was a good thing. I just had to turn it around. The immediate frustration lasted as long as New Year's Day. I sat on my own on the sofa and I was like, *This is not what I signed up for.* At the time it couldn't be shittier. I didn't even get the injury in competition, I got the injury while having a *walk.* It's like you're at your most vulnerable when your guard is down.

I knew I had to turn it around. First things first. How do we fix the problem? There's actually very little you can do to speed up the healing process of an injury, especially if you put snowboarding into the mix. It wasn't going to help, but I didn't really have a choice. The fear was that I would risk being in the same situation as before, having to qualify six weeks before the Olympics. I thought, *Let's get back into competition as soon as possible*, but the next competition was only two weeks later. Was that a smart decision? Well, maybe not. I competed in Kreischberg 14 days after the injury. I was back in the place where I could build my confidence up – a competitive environment. It's aggressive, it's harsh, it's brash and, even though everyone is nice to each other, it's still competitive. It doesn't matter what the weather is doing. On a normal training day, you can look at the conditions and say, *Meh, I don't fancy it today*. On competition day, I really didn't fancy it but I couldn't risk repeating what had happened in 2013 at the previous Olympic qualifiers. I wasn't going to let that happen again. So this time I was like, *Right, let's be having it*. I was a woman on a mission.

There was a really big question as to the load and the impact that I could personally deal with. I had no faith in the ability of my ankle. That part of my body wasn't working to full capacity. I didn't trust it. So, it was going to be about how strong my pain threshold was. And would I make my ankle worse? Would it be better to wait another week or should I ride through it and just get points? These were the questions going through my head and the physios were saying, 'Well, it's not going to be great, but if you want to compete we will tape it up and see what you can do.'

My physio Mary was amazing. She was a really strong, very knowledgeable Austrian woman who had dealt with a lot of ankle, wrist and knee injuries. She was based at a clinic in Innsbruck and she made me feel confident that I was in good hands. But, magic as they are, physios cannot make pain disappear. I remember her strapping my ankle and just lightly touching it. I shrieked and burst into tears with the pain. It was so raw. Still, I joined my practice run. I was able to go up and just watch everybody else. The one blessing I clung to was the fact that I had ridden that course before. It was a course I didn't particularly like, but it was a course that I had ridden. I'd been here before.

I was taking every little grain of positivity to provide comfort to my situation. I'd ridden the course before. I'd done a lot of snowboarding. I told myself lots of positive things. I had to. I had the ability to just watch and rock up and do it. I knew I could visualize it. I could pretend I was riding this course. I had lots of experience to lean on and just had to believe through visualization that it was possible. On the day, I just rocked up and did it. I literally winged it. Yes, it was a little bit dangerous, but I knew I had the ability to grin and bear it. It was literally a case of surviving the course and getting some points on the board, but I was in agony. I remember landing – it was my back foot; the pain was raw. It was jagged. It was killing me when I was walking, but I couldn't let my mind give in. I told myself, *It's not a problem. I know it's there, but I'll deal with it later.* A weakness and an injury. It never goes away. There's a memory in your body and there's a slight doubt in your mind that it's not as strong as it once was. It's not even in the same position. It is damaged.

I guess it's all about trust. The first time you put weight on an injured limb, bone or muscle, you have to deal with the fear that it won't work and that means rebuilding trust. I've had injuries that were painful to ride on, but this was a new kind of pain. It was the emotional pain that this was not how or who I wanted to be. I couldn't allow myself to be in this negative state. I had to flip everything. I had to be like, *Okay, I did it.* I took one step closer rather than one step back.

The next qualifier event was about a week later at Laax. I'd survived the first one, but this course in Switzerland is one of the biggest Slopestyle courses in the world. It's really long and the way it is situated, you can't just ride the course; you have to go all the way down the mountain and get the chairlift back up. So, I was on my feet a whole lot more than I was in Krieschberg. There, you just do the run and you're at the bottom. Whereas Laax is a top-to-bottom run with a five-minute ski run at the end of it, so the time on my feet and the pressure on my ankle were so much greater. The environment just didn't lend itself to allowing me to have any recovery time. I thought *I'll just do it. I'll wing it.* I went up. Came down super-low in the field. Survived. Still, I was point collecting, but I was way down: fortieth place.

It was no surprise that I didn't make the semi-finals, but from then on I just started focusing on my recovery. Rather than bashing my ankle, I was going to the pool. I was stretching. I was doing yoga and started visualizing what the ankle would be like when it was better. I started visualizing what I wanted to achieve the following week. I did a lot of water therapy. I stayed content in my environment in Laax and took faith that I'd be a lot stronger and a lot better for my next competition. I was still in agony, but it was a pain I could deal with so I could get it taped up in order to board. Before, I would have just shied away from it and gone, *No, I'm not doing that*. This was a much more mature approach in the face of fear. The fear of injury. The fear of pain. I managed to train a bit, but mainly rested the ankle.

That qualifier in Laax proved to me that sometimes just riding the course is all you can do, but you still need to do it. Even with a battered ankle, I could compete. I knew how to ride a course and could work out how to prepare for the future, despite a limiting injury. Just turning up, going through the motions, was, at some level, the qualifying run. I learned that I wasn't bulletproof. I wasn't immune to injury. I had to operate within the known limits of my ability at that time.

By the end of the season, I was ranked fifth in Slopestyle and third in Big Air. My World Cup qualification prospects in 2014 and 2018 were like the difference between day and night. Three-and-a-half weeks after the injury, my ankle was on the mend, giving me back the ability to ride. It was still painful, but nothing like the two events beforehand had been; I was blown away by what the body can do. This was the World Cup, Seiser Alm, Italy. I went there and ended up coming fifth overall. After that, give or take a gammy ankle, the rest of the season was stong – back-to-back top-5 results and a 4th place in the Czech Republic meant it was pretty certain I'd secured my place at the PyeongChang Olympics. It wasn't official, but it felt like such a relief. I could relax. I was in a happier place. I was content in my performance and my abilities. I'd achieved what I'd set out to do, which was the best feeling ever. This is where I was meant to be and – for that extra feeling of triumph – I had got there despite starting the year with a ruptured ligament.

So I thought, *I've qualified. What could possibly go wrong?* In snowboarding, quite a lot really. You are only as good as your last competition. Injury became a huge worry because I wanted to go to the Olympics so much. I started getting scared and it wasn't just fear of injury, it was fear of missing out. I really struggled with motivation, because I was worried about getting hurt. There's so much in snowboarding which is about doing it because you love it but I had reached a place where I wasn't loving it any more. What I came to learn was it's okay not to enjoy it all the time. I had a job to do. I had to go and get on with it. And that's what I did.

14

WHEN IT'S TIME TO WALK AWAY

In November 2017, I had a block of training in Austria. Standing at the top of a slope at what was meant to be a training camp for the Olympics, I knew I didn't want to be there. I would go up the mountain and I would burst into tears. I'd literally hide the tears behind my goggles. I didn't feel happy on my board. I wasn't enjoying it. I was scared. I was really, really scared. It hadn't been announced yet, but I had qualified for the 2018 Olympics. To be in that position so far in advance was a positive thing, but I didn't *feel* positive within myself. I'd also split up with my boyfriend of four-and-a-half years and my nan had been diagnosed with cancer. Looking back, I used those trigger points, those life events, as reasons to excuse myself from performing. While those life curveballs did have a huge impact, I also used splitting up with my boyfriend as an excuse for why I was really sad. Deep down, I knew it wasn't that. It wasn't that at all. I was scared of hurting myself before the Olympics. I was very good at masking it. I just didn't really want to be doing this. It was pure fear.

My physio had been working with me for years. I got on with her so well and she knew everything. Every intimate detail. She recommended that I have some sessions with the psychologist and I thought *why not?* It was my first time talking to a mental-health professional, so it was quite a big step for me to even entertain that it might be useful. So I had a chat. I told her there's a lot of shit going on in my life and it has been distracting me, but what it really boils down to is I'm just scared. I said, 'I just want to survive this, to get it done, so I can do what I really want to do.' I was done with snowboarding. I hated it. I just wanted to do enough to go to the PyeongChang Olympics, so I could earn a living out of it and use the brand I'd created to go into what I really wanted to do. In essence, my passion had changed and I was fearful because what I was doing wasn't serving me any more.

The pyschologist was like, 'Well, that's fine.' So I said, 'I'm telling you, I really, really, really want to stop this and you're telling me that's okay, because I want to use it to take me somewhere else?' Then she paid me a massive compliment. She said of all the athletes she had met, I was one of the most aware of my mental thought process. She said I didn't need a psychologist, I just needed to know that what I was thinking was okay. The takeaway from that one session was it's okay to *not* love what you're doing. I could feel the pressure fall from my shoulders, because I had always carried the belief that you *have* to love what you do if you want to succeed. There's no question that if you need to reach a specific goal, intrinsic motivation will serve you better than any other motivation. But if it will take you to where you want to go, it's okay to use what you *ultimately* want as your motivation to get you through.

At a time when you need energy and drive, you have to find the thing that will serve you the most. For me, that was knowing that by keeping going, by riding through, by pushing on, by being on the mountain and not doing anything stupid, I would get to where I wanted to be. So, I just had to just keep on going.

If you really want the goal beyond the goal, you need to show up. For me, there's always been this Catch-22: if you don't practise, you might not get there, but if you practise too much, you might not be there at all.

There have been many times when I have turned things round in my brain and found the motivation to go back up the mountain. I just wasn't always ecstatic about doing it. However, I vividly recall two events which didn't pan out like that at all. Two moments stick out in my mind when I went to the top of the jump, looked down and just didn't want to do it. I just burst into tears. Because there are times when you need to listen to a deeper truth.

In the build-up to the 2018 Olympics in PyeongChang, I drove to Italy for the World Cup. I'd had a really good year there in 2017. It was the first Olympic qualifier and I had come fifth in the finals. I was absolutely buzzing. All of that season was a great year for me. Fast forward to one year later: I arrived and I was like, *I've already done what I did last year, so I'm just here to be a part of it all*. I thought I could just knuckle down. I would practise, go to bed, get an early night. But there were a few tricks that I needed to do that I was fearful of, and I just didn't feel up to it. So, instead of dealing with it and doing some practice, I just sort of sat around and distracted myself. I just pulled the goggles down. I just thought, *I'm really upset* and I blamed it on everything else that was going on. The boyfriend. My nan. I didn't really deal with it at all, but I got through it, did the competition and did as much as I was comfortable with. In ladder terms, I was sticking around five, six, seven because I didn't want to risk going any higher. Staying in my comfort zone meant I was going to do what I was going to do. No more, no less. I was okay with that. But it wasn't really good enough. Nor was it really facing up to what was going on in my head. I thought going to the Olympics was the most important thing, because that served my bigger goal, yet it was creating a whole new fear in me. I was scared of being hurt and failing in my goal.

There was another time, in Mönchengladbach, Germany, where I had the same feeling. There was no pressure. I'd been there the year before. I was actually in a place where I could just turn up and cruise. Because there was no pressure to deliver, I thought *why not save it for when it really matters?* Right? Wrong! The best practice protocol would be to go through the course and ride it like a competition. Step out of my comfort zone. Climb the ladder up to eight, nine, ten. Get used to being at the top. But when I got to the top of the course, I looked down and lost it. I remember just turning round, getting in the lift and going back down to the bottom of the jump. A voice in my head was saying, *Aimee what are you doing? This is not you. You need to keep going.*

You can't throw the towel in. This is not going to serve you later down the line, if you turn up unprepared. I told myself to get my shit together. *Go back up!*

One part of me was thinking, *No, it's all right, chill.* But the other part was saying, *Aimee, you absolute moron, go back up there – you have to hit the jump – go and get your air miles! It's just air miles.* The minute I made the goal approachable, broke it into its component parts, I was up for it. But the blocks and mental barriers were there with the bigger tricks and they were going to come home to roost at the Olympics. This was something ever-present now. Once I decided my goal wasn't to be a snowboarder, the inner motivation fell apart. This wasn't something that I could resolve. Once I became afraid of hurting myself and once that fear got too great, I lost interest. Simply put, it got too hairy for me and snowboarding success was no longer the goal. I wanted to move on to the next thing.

*

PYEONGCHANG, SOUTH KOREA, 2018

It was the first time that Big Air was in the Olympics. I was on my third of five practice runs before the competition. I was at the top of the ramp, ready to go, when I realized my bindings had broken. *Shit.*

Bindings are the rubber bungees that hold your boots onto the snowboard. You'd think, it's the Olympics, Aimee, surely you should have some spare? But here's the thing – deep down in my mind I was thinking, *I don't need spares because I'm not going to do anything that's going to break them. That would be far too dangerous. I might hurt myself and then I'd have to miss the competition.* To deal with a very real, stomach-churning, broken-neck, me-in-a-wheelchair fear, I was thinking, *These bindings have been good for so long, why would I have a spare set? I'm so on top of my shit, I don't need spare bindings.* Duh.

My signature trick is a cab double nine hundred: you have to go down the ramp backwards, hit the jump and as you go off the jump you turn 180°, do a double backflip and land facing forward. I had only managed to do it once in the practice sessions beforehand. I had waited until the very last minute, I did it once and I landed it. Maybe if I had done it at the start of the training, it would have cleared the way for putting in more practice, but I was afraid of getting hurt in the practice and missing the competition. I wasn't comfortable enough. So it was more measured. I thought,

This is what I'm doing. I didn't want to do it in practice. I thought I needed the fuel of the competition to do it. But there's no question about it, I was scared.

Weather conditions, especially the wind, in PyeongChang had been really bad, and a lot of people had already ended up in hospital. Now, I could do the single in my sleep. I could do the single in any environment, but as soon as you throw in a few environmental curveballs – snow, wind, ice, the size of the jump – the double suddenly feels further away. It's doable, but harder to access. Harder to get out of the trick bag. It was my fault. I had trained and trained and trained doing the single repeatedly, but I didn't want to practise the double because I felt uncomfortable on that jump. So I didn't have much practice on it and I knew I didn't have enough time to get into cruise control for going upside-down twice. I was afraid of it.

My approach in the past had been to get a trick so comfortable that I could get into cruise control. This time, I had enough respect for the double, especially in this environment, that I knew I ran the risk of the kind of serious injury that would take me out of the competition. No doubt. There's a time and a place for feeling excitement about the unknown, and that's when you can step up to the challenge. This time, I didn't have that feeling, the buzz of the unknown. It wasn't excitement any more. It was fear.

You get five practice runs before the contest. This was the bit I liked. A little bit of pressure before the competition. *Okay, Aimee, it's go time.* Run one. I drop in straight. Fair. Drop in for run two. Do the switch single once. I've got three goes to play with. It's now or never to do the double. I've got to get this. I've got to get this board over my head twice. Run number three. *Deep breath. God, I'm scared. No, you've got this, you're ready, you're prepped, you've done this so many times on the airbag.* Drop in. Toe, heel, explode. Round once, twice, grab the board, land it. Holy shit! I've done it. I've landed it! What a relief. I'm thinking, *Wow if I land this again, I could get into the finals.* I unstrap my binding and walk back up to the top of the ramp. And that's when I realize that my binding is broken.

I've still got 20 minutes before the contest starts, so I slide down the ramp and go to my coach. He says, 'Don't worry, I'll get mine.' I've always been particular about things around my feet. When I was four, I had a pair of Converse and the laces were a nightmare because I needed them doing up just right. 'Mummy, do them tighter, they're not tight enough!' It used to drive my mum mad. Anyway, the coach puts his bindings on my board. They're fatter, the thickness isn't right. I'm up next. I freak out. 'No. That's not good enough.' I should have known better. I have never, ever felt like this. I've heard people talk about the pressure being overwhelming, but my attitude had always been that I never wanted it to define me. But here it is – the pressure they talk about. It's now. It's happening to me now. At the Olympics.

I see Jess, my Australian mate, and I say, 'Have you got two boards? Have you got two sets of bindings? Can I have one of your straps?' And she says, 'Yes, go, it's down at the bottom.' Then it's, 'Last runs, everyone!' and I'm seriously flustered. I'm slightly cold because I've been standing around, but I've also got a bit of a sweat on because I'm so nervous. I'm feeling rigid. I had such a high from landing that double that my blood sugar has now plummeted, my heart rate has gone from through the roof to really low and my adrenal system is upside-down. I'm thinking, *Why has this happened to me? I was feeling good. Everything was going in the right direction. Why has this happened?*

I get the board strapped on. I get to the top of the jump. I'm the last to drop. The whole field of 32 girls has gone already and I'm the last one to drop on the last practice run.

I fling myself off the jump. I ride down. Let's just say I'm in nervous cruise control. I do a single. Didn't grab it. I didn't do anything. I was like one of those chewy penny sweets, stretched but all brittle. That's how my body had gone.

So, that was it. Then…showtime. The broadcast was on and we were going live in 16 minutes. I made my way back up the steps and tried to stay in the zone. I was thinking, *It doesn't matter, whatever it is, it'll be fine. You can do this. Remember the training. Forget about the last jump. That doesn't matter. It's not going to contribute to the bigger picture. Just forget about it.*

I am standing at the top and they call my name. I am looking down into the Olympic Stadium in PyeongChang at the first ever Big Air event at the Olympics. I check my bindings about six times. I have this nervous tic, tail-to-nose, tail-to-nose, tail- to-nose, that I do about six times. I look down at the jump. Take a few deep breaths and I drop in. First time, I get it right, I'm thinking *toe heel, toe heel, explode, one, two, this is working.* I almost panic, I am so shocked that it is working. I touch down, both feet instantaneously, stomp it, almost perfect. And then I fall over. I just lose it.

I was like, *Aimee! What are you doing? It was there!* I had just done it. Literally, my feet touched the ground, but it was as though my legs were made out of strawberry laces. My body just shut down. My legs were done. I was like, *oh my God!*

I thought, *It's okay, you've got one more to go.* The truth was, apart from falling over, everything else had gone right. Toe, heel, explode, one rotation, two rotations, spot the landing. It was almost like I had been in shock that I pulled it off because of what had happened in the practice run: the stress around the binding, the anxiety and the overwhelming stomach-churning fear, along with being cold and feeling stiff. I'd almost mentally prepared not to land the double, so when I did I had crumbled under the pressure. I was so shocked that it was going my way, because the actions and the emotions that had happened just beforehand had left me unprepared to pull it off.

Everything else up to this moment had been positive. *You can do it. What's the worst thing that can happen?* Yet, in that moment of the broken binding, the coach offering up a solution and me saying it wasn't good enough, it seems a negative process happened that I'd never encountered before. It was like I was realizing, this is not the one. This is not the day. In a sense, I'd always tried never to build the Olympics up to be bigger than any other competition. But in reality, deep down, I truly knew that it was. So, maybe it was the sudden realization that this *did* mean a lot more to me than I thought? I don't know. There were so many different thoughts going on inside my head. It was as if I was searching for an excuse, then internalizing it and trying so hard to be okay with all of it.

But then I had a sudden feeling that this moment is *now*. This moment *needs* me to stay present. I knew that, at the end of the day, I didn't want this event to define me. I guess that was me looking to the bigger picture. I know that I was putting it in perspective. My mum and dad were watching. They were okay. My nan and grandad had flown all the way to Korea. I didn't total myself and end up in hospital after my first run, that had been one of my fears. There were so many different emotions going on inside my head and everything turned against me in that moment.

With my classic sense of positive self, I was like, *Okay let's go to the top and have another go!* I was trying to convince myself that it was okay, but I didn't believe that it would be. That's when the shit really hit the fan. It was the pressure. The idea that this is your last chance, and if you don't land this you're out of the competition. This particular moment was either going to catapult me into the finals and it was going to be the best Olympics ever, or it was going to be the last jump of my career because I was ready to move on. I was done with it. I was done with the pressure and the anxiety and stress of performing and I had other ambitions. Maybe, psychologically, at a really deep level in my head I sort of knew that was it. I knew I was done with this and so did the people very close to me; my mum and dad. I was done.

But before that second jump there was something deeper going on, something that meant I was already moving on. This time, I was listening to myself and trusting my instincts. I knew there were a couple of times when I'd ignored those feelings, used a shady excuse, like it's my boyfriend or some bad family news, but subconsciously I was thinking, *Once I've done this, it's job done. So, let's get it over with.*

Right now, I was at the top of the jump. It sucked. So, I dropped in and I got the movement pattern wrong. This time I went heel to heel. Essentially, I crumpled. I was upside-down. I was out of control. It was as if someone had shot me out of a cannon. I got the take-off wrong and I was sort of rigid, like a piece of dry spaghetti. I went all long and thin and stiff. I was bracing myself for impact. I literally landed headfirst in the ground. I remember at that moment thinking, *Shit, you idiot.* At the same time, I literally pushed up with my hands and touched my breasts to check they were still there because I'd smashed them into the ground. I touched my face. It was okay. I got up, took my board off and I was just smiling. I was like, *that's it. It's done. You're okay. On to the next thing.* I've never been upside-down twice since.

*

Looking back on it now, if I was to give myself advice, I'd say you *do* need to over-prepare. I'd also say never let your equipment be your excuse. I'd pulled off the double in practice and then the whole drama and fear around the binding had disrupted my routine. It distracted me sufficiently to pull me out of my fully focused flow state. It was actually like someone walking into the room and farting when you're trying to concentrate, when you're trying to meditate. This disruption to the process that I had planned in my head broke the pattern, and because the pattern had been thrown out of whack, I didn't have the ability to regain control of it. I almost gave up, but I'm glad I completed that last run.

After that, my goal became to present at the Olympics,

not compete in them. I didn't let that run define me because I'd already decided that I was on the next chapter. I'd commentated at the Sochi Olympics in 2014 and knew the rush of live broadcast, especially in the commentary box. The Olympics was a perfect opportunity for me. I knew the spirit of the games, the environment and how fantastic this sport could be. And then the opportunity had presented itself. Presenting the next day with the BBC, I'm sure many people would have seen me and thought, 'Here's a blonde-haired snowboarder who wants a bit of telly time', but it was more than that. I came in, I was early. I sat there and chatted to everyone – engaged with everyone. I wanted to know how it all happened, how to do it, and how to improve. I had already run away with my thoughts on the next step of my journey.

Since the last day I dropped in at the 2018 Olympics in PyeongChang, everything I have done has been geared towards gaining an awareness and understanding of the knowledge and experience required to hold the microphone and develop my broadcast career.

I'd gone from someone who dreamed of being able to snowboard to becoming a professional. My passion had become my whole way of life. It became my job and, after a while, it was a job I was done with. I learned that life's greatest passion can also become its enemy if overconsumed. That translates to food, drink and all sorts of other things. Even exercise! This is stuff I've never really voiced. I've never spoken about this before, because I'd never wanted it to be my excuse, but at the end of the day, the passion was gone for me.

*

I got to experience the glory years of snowboarding. I had a good three-and-a-half year run before the Sochi 2014 Olympics were even on my radar. So I got a taste of what snowboarding really was about. The rock'n'roll. The culture. The magazines and the videos. These days, a lot of it is about Instagram and commercial deals, but back then it was simply about who got the best shot – it was about being stoked. Slopestyle, the type of snowboarding I did, wasn't even in the Olympics back then! It didn't matter. I knew I could make a career out of it and slopestylers didn't need to aim for the Olympics, because we had our own thing going on. There was enough of a world tour. There were opportunities for a hundred grand prize money and being sponsored by top brands. It was its own thing.

Most snowboarders are not okay with retiring. They see snowboarding as a permanent way of life and they're not in it to retire. But I wasn't like that. My attitude to snowboarding has always been as simple as: I like it and I want to do it. I liked that, at the grassroots level, there was no one to tell you what to do, and I chose snowboarding over gymnastics partly because gymnastics was a bit militant, whereas when I got into snowboarding it was all about play and creativity. When I realized the degree of practice and training required to go pro, I had the wiring in place to understand the why and the how of practice. But once I decided I was done with it, I also felt the freedom to walk away.

That's partly because the energy around snowboarding is really positive. We talk about things being rad, being stoked on landing a new trick. That largely defined the environment. It wasn't until much later, after the Olympics, when there was a new sense of finality, that the stoked feeling became too obscured by fear, and that's when I knew I was done.

15

IT'S A MARATHON, NOT A SPRINT

I had always wondered what it would be like to run a marathon and the perfect time to do it was the year after the PyeongChang Olympics. I could never have done it before, because of the way snowboarding mashes your body. The Olympics was like my graduation. I never went to university. This was my degree. The feeling afterwards was, *I've done it. I've done it twice. I don't need to put myself through that again. Cool, what's next?* I wanted to explore the unknown with no real set purpose, other than doing things that I was interested in and passionate about. So, in a way, it gave me the space to put my energy into finding different ways to push my body.

The fact that my first marathon was in North Korea, to

film a documentary for the Olympic Channel, just made the whole thing all the more exciting. Bear in mind that this was my first marathon ever. The physical running part was straightforward in itself. My motivation was also straightforward. I just needed to get through this so that in two weeks' time I could be in London, where I was due to run the London Marathon with my mum. It was the complete opposite of the physical and mental preparation needed for a professional snowboarding competition. My thinking was, *It can't be anywhere near as scary or difficult as turning myself upside-down two-and-a-half times when it's -40 degrees.* I was used to being at seven, eight, nine on the ladder – high up on the scale of fear – and the real danger of running was around level three. While there was a sense of fear about being in North Korea itself, a few butterflies over the sense of the unknown, I stripped the race itself back to the simplicity of doing something that I could already do. I was just repeating it and repeating it for a sustained period of time. There was nothing unknown about it, other than a new physical territory that I had never been to. But there was no ladder required for the task itself. It was a pure mental skill.

My bigger fear was fear of missing out. The concern that

I would hurt myself and not be available to run the marathon in London with my mum. I had committed to do something and I'm very strong on the commitment front. I don't like letting people down. If it's just myself, I'm okay but if there's someone else involved, I hold myself to a high level of accountability. I didn't want my mum running her first marathon by herself. I wanted to be there with her, so my biggest fear going to North Korea was getting injured and leaving my mum to go through our marathon alone. It was a serious concern.

To be totally honest, I had never been able to run more than three miles due to tendonitis and bruised heels. Because of snowboarding, I've got really messed-up feet, so the question was: how do I make sure they survive the race? Mentally, I scaled it right back and pretended there were a few less miles than there really were. I made the goal smaller and broke it down into a series of tiny steps. Really tiny in my case. I started with two-and-a-half miles in December, by Christmas I was running seven, by January thirteen and by February I managed nineteen miles. Then in March, I was on the plane to North Korea. When you've got 26 miles to run, you really do have to break down every single step. In my mind, each step I took was chipping away at the marathon, taking me one step closer to the goal that I had in mind. It was my motivation to keep going.

Sometimes, if your goal is not about achieving your best performance, but simply completing a task, distraction is a great accomplice. My distractions were that we were filming a documentary, I was meeting Korean athletes and I was in such a strange environment that the task of running in an actual marathon was really quite simple compared with the logistical challenges of different food, different culture, different kinds of people, a strange hotel and no freedom.

The North Korean athletes put it all into perspective for me. They were so lean and so fit and they were running in plimsolls. Literally in the plimsolls that we used to use for PE when we were four years old. And I had trainers with cells made with lasers. They only had one tracksuit each. I remember when they said, 'Our tracksuit is our uniform.' Being an athlete was their trade and that was what they wore to work. The other thing that was touching was they all had these handmade cloth bags – the type that you get in boutique bakers or book shops – and they recorded their training schedules in pencil in tiny columns in thin notebooks. No digital technology. No apps.

It made me realize that we have so much stuff, so much clutter in Western society and it really brought home the fact that we don't need all these material things. Don't get me wrong, I'm glad we have them, because they do enhance performance, but the North Koreans prove that it's possible to compete on the world stage without all of this stuff. Let's just say, I realized we are so blessed with the resources and the sports technology that we have. I wasn't capitalizing on their misfortune, but I was counting my blessings. Through being abroad and travelling, it was natural to make comparisons. It was incredibly humbling, but also enabling. *If they can do it, I can do it.* It was about perspective. There was no reason why I couldn't run this marathon.

The biggest fear I had was the underlying fear of something going wrong. Simply being in a country 'shrouded in mystery' can easily get you caught up in the headspace of *what if, what if, what if?* Whatever. You have to park *what if*, because there is nothing you can do about it. We really were going into uncharted territory and there was only so much I could do if anything went wrong.

There are things within your control and things outside your control, and what I could control was pretty basic. I'd been to South Korea. I'd been to China. I knew that they didn't really do porridge as I understood it. So, I took some oats and I found a way to microwave them. I made sure I had the right shoes and I got my own water bottle. I had specific things to focus on, but the environment was so foreign that I made the bigger picture pretty simple too. Get out of the gate and put one foot in front of the other. Just keep going, because the truth is, I am so blessed. Movement is a gift and not everyone has it. So, come on, get going. One foot in front of the other. It really was that simple in my head.

I think we can often overlook the gifts we are given. Control the things you can control, but don't obsess over them. I brought a few things with me to make me feel comfortable, but they weren't going to affect whether I could put one foot in front of the other or how I would cope when it got tough – because I knew it was going to get tough, especially around mile 19. So how was I going to get through it? It came back to the constant inner thought process; talking to myself.

The day of the race came around. It was beautifully

sunny and yet bitingly cold. I was around 15 miles in, on what seemed like the longest road. So, there were about 11 miles to go. My knee hurt. I had never felt pain like it. I was thinking, *Is this an okay pain? Is this normal? Do I need to stop? Or is it not too bad? Let's just keep going . . .* but then it worsened. I had this constant chatter. *Is it bad? Is it not bad? Is it okay? Will I be able to walk in two days' time?* I was caught in a consuming state of physical awareness. I was trying to talk myself out of the pain and into the feeling I would have at the end of the race: I had never run a marathon; I was about to complete my first one. I was trying to hold on to the thought of how lucky I was to be able to run. *I've done 15 miles, only 11 to go.*

One of the skills I've developed is the ability to compartmentalize my thoughts and assess them. So, if you come across a positive thought in a difficult time, hold that thought in the centre of your consciousness. If a thought comes into your head that's negative – and there are going to be plenty of negative ones during something that's as physically demanding as a marathon – just allow them to pass through. Let the negative thoughts flow freely. This is the complete opposite to the approach of so many athletes, trainers and coaches, who seem to think you should just suck it up or suppress the negative thoughts. I always find it easier to allow them in and let them go.

While the negative thoughts come in my left ear and go out of my right ear, I imagine the positive thought is stuck on my forehead on a sticky Post-It note. Higher up in my brain map, I focus on the good one and let the others just flow past.

But this pain? It hurt. It hurt a lot. The worst moment was around mile 19. The fear was simple. There was still so far to go and my right knee was banjaxed. This was a different pain to anything I'd experienced before. I never had problems with my knees. My ankles have had problems, but this was a new kind of pain. The knee pain was different. When the documentary crew pulled up alongside, filming me from the mini-van, there was a part of me that wanted to just get in.

I felt like I was hobbling. In my mind I was hobbling. But I knew that I had to shift my perspective. I thought, *If this is as bad as it gets, there are a lot more things in life and in the world that are worse.* So, the pain was on board. I couldn't really get rid of it, so I needed to accept it. But I didn't want the pain to be a negative. Never let pain define you. Accept it and work out how to keep on riding through it. Don't let it be something that stops you because, at the end of the day, that's what pain can do. It can stop you from achieving your goal. So, I had to accept it, process it and allow it on board. But I didn't allow it to be at the front and centre of my mind map. I held the good feelings at the front of my mind: the feeling of finishing and the sense of accomplishment I would feel.

The challenge was all about not letting pain override my positive thoughts. I couldn't let the negative thoughts stop me from achieving what I wanted. The fact that I was being filmed meant I didn't feel totally alone. The presence of the film crew reminded me that I was doing this for everyone else. I could have hopped into the crew's van at any moment, but I made do with being tossed a banana and some water. I didn't get in the van, because that wasn't my role. I had a different part to play. It was important to do this for myself, as well as for the film crew.

One of the hacks I have used to help realize my goals is to use pressure effectively. There are two types of pressure: external and internal, and I often use a combination of both. When I was running the marathon in North Korea, there were people who were depending on me to run the marathon and, because of those bonds, I felt a pressure inside to deliver; not just for myself, but as part of the wider team.

My options were really quite limited now; suck it up and get on with it or be a failure. And I kind of liked being in that environment. There was no real recipe, no secret bag of tricks. It was just about survival. Get through it. Simple. The day before, my mum had run 22 miles and I drew on that. I dug in and put one foot in front of the other. It hurt, but I reasoned there was no point at which I was going to render myself permanently injured and need to spend the rest of my life in a wheelchair – or in fact die – all of which had been possibilities in snowboarding.

To be honest, I'm not a runner. And to put it in perspective, the level of actual fear that I was operating in was probably around about three on my ladder. Sometimes, it's hard to break down the individual steps, the individual mini-goals that take you to the ultimate goal. This was not one of those occasions. Running is simple. And I kept on reminding myself of that through the race. One foot in front of the other.

But the fear for me was this: can my body deal with this physical load for a long period of time? I was worried my body wouldn't let me do it, that my physical fitness would let me down. Coming from a sport like snowboarding, your body takes a fair amount of impact. Physically, it's all about fast-twitch muscle fibre, so in long-distance running I was coming to a different sport. I didn't want my body breaking down to be an excuse. I knew I wasn't expected to be running particularly fast, so my focus was more about survival and knowing that ten days later I was going to have to do it again in a different time zone, at the London Marathon with my mum. I was not just doing one marathon, but doing two, back-to-back, and suddenly this felt like a big physical load for my body. I didn't want to let Mum down. I didn't want to turn up in London and go, *Sorry, Mum, I can't run because my knees are broken.*

All these mental anxieties were tugging at me numerous times during the race, but I remembered the importance of allowing negativity into my brain, so that I could just let it flow through, pick it up and throw it out. It's a mental process and it's a constant, rhythmic patter. Remember why you're doing it, remember what you're doing it for. Look to the end point and picture the feeling you're going to get from doing it. It's not like you sit cross-legged before the race and meditate. But you can still prepare mentally. You can visualize.

As you undertake any challenge, a ton of negative thoughts, statements and fears will pop up. So, in North Korea, when I started running, there was the fear that I wouldn't complete the marathon and then I had another fear that I was going to let people down. Even before this, there was a more fundamental fear – what if I can't do it? One of the first things to do is neutralize those fears. In my head, there's a softer side which says, *It doesn't matter if you can't do it.* To help deflate that pressure and to relieve the performance anxiety on myself, I'll just go out and do what I can do and that makes it more approachable.

So, by the time I came to the starting line, there wasn't the gut-wrenching fear of performance. The pressure was still there – I was aware of it – but for me it was all about survival, and my best this time was just getting through it, because that's all I needed to do.

Then, I've got to get through the process. That's when the 'what if' fears arise. In the marathon, for me specifically, it was my feet. *What if my feet get such savage pins and needles I can barely feel my toes?* I'd heard there are moments running a marathon when that might come up. So, I think, *Okay, I've thought about this beforehand, so here it is. I'm just going to forget about it. I'm going to pick it up and throw it out.*

There are the feelings before the race – the anxiety, the nerves, the fear of not being able to do it. Then there are the feelings during the race – *this is painful, this is a struggle* and the fear of not breaking through. Then there are the feelings after the race – the sense of accomplishment, the physical feeling of completing something, the mental feeling of completing something, of accomplishing a goal – that in itself is a mental elation and high. When you complete a goal, there's a real buzz and that's the main feeling – because I can tell you the physical feeling after doing a marathon isn't great – but mentally knowing that your body has done that, it's like *wow!*

So, there are three clear phases, but you have to think about each one before it happens. When you're in each phase, you need to recognize the pattern. Some of those phases may or may not feel different to what you imagined, but it helps for you to stay with it anyway. So, let's take the fear of my body giving up. There was a really bad feeling in my right knee with six miles to go but, because I anticipated that fear, I could handle it. It's like, *Okay, that's one of my concerns, here's the feeling, I recognize it, now I need to approach and deal with it*. If I just suddenly had the feeling, *Oh, my knee hurts*, then I'd be more likely to panic and freak out and would end up feeling like I had to give up.

So, when I was running the marathon and the pain came into my knees, 26.2 miles felt impossible. But it's all relative. Goals are relative to the time you're in, to time periods and timeframes. It's about managing the experience – if you're expecting it, you can accept it and if you can accept it, you can move on from it. The voice in my head was going, *Here it comes! Oh shit! It's worse than I thought!* But then, there's another part of me which is saying, *Aimee, stop being a pussy and get on with it!* I find that giving myself a strict talking-to can, in some situations, be as valid in dealing with fear as using my softer side. It is actually all about tone of voice. If I think my body is giving up, there are different tones of voice I can use to help focus on the bigger picture, while breaking the goal into manageable steps.

*

I still find I use this method of one foot in front of the other, breaking things down into manageable steps, in every area of my life. Recently my tendonitis returned in my big toe joint and I really wasn't able to run. (I think it's actually a repetitive strain injury from the 2.6 Charity Challenge I did during lockdown: 26 backflips in my back garden.) Anyway, I hurt my big toe. I had just started running again and my calves felt tired. The goal in my head was: *I really want to do 5k.* So, I thought, *Why not just go out and do a mile?* But once I was into it, I thought, *Well, let's do another one.* I'd taken the fear out of it. I mentally eased myself into running again by removing expectation, and that helped to make it more approachable. I was gentle with myself. I broke it down. One step at a time.

It is fine to have a big goal, but what I have learned is that if you want to help overcome your mental obstacles to reaching that goal, it's vital to have achievable landmarks along the way. You don't climb the mountain in one giant leap. You reach the top through a series of small steps. It's vital that these can be scaled up or scaled down.

Say you have an immediate goal for exercise, but you don't have a lot of time. I always wanted to get a good hour of exercise in when I was on tour. But sometimes with flight times, jet lag and competition schedules, I knew that getting that hour in the morning might have actually taken away from the greater need of getting proper rest. So, I learned to scale things down. If you haven't got an hour, take 40 minutes. Or break it into 30 minutes in the morning and 30 in the evening. Maybe you haven't got time for 30 minutes in the morning? Take 20. Something is always better than nothing.

When you are looking at longer-term goals, you always need to break them down into several mini-hurdles. By breaking the big thing into several smaller, more achievable steps, you can gradually scale the bigger goal. I always put several mini-hurdles together into a series. Sometimes, you clear fewer, sometimes more. But if you put the right steps in place, you will progress along the course.

16

MANIFESTING A
NEW DIRECTION

It's a given that we have to put ourselves in certain situations to make the things we want happen; 99.9 per cent of the goals I've achieved have been down to rigorous time management. But controlling time brings with it the risk that you don't leave any time for yourself. As the great Chris Fuller says, 'The best time you can have is the time that you can waste.' My dad loves a deep dive – in fact, he's peppered my life with profound one-liners. But this is the one I should probably have inked on my butt cheek: the best time is time you have to kill. Free time, the time when you're bored, that really is the best time. But what if all you have is free time?

Before the COVID-19 pandemic, I was burning the candle at both ends and in the middle. One minute I was hosting a yoga retreat, the next minute I was in Estonia presenting. Before I knew it, I was on another flight back to the UK, to then hop on an overnight bus to film a BBC feature travelling to Austria. It felt like I was on a treadmill, I'd pressed the turbo button, I was on the incline, *and* juggling three different things. There was so much going on that I didn't really have time to process the direction of my actions, where they would take me, and what I really wanted to achieve. It was just end-to-end motion and action. And then it stopped.

The pandemic made me take my foot off the gas. After doing seven flights in a week, juggling multiple jobs, I think I'd hit that point…I was burned out. The opportunity to go home and be in one place for more than four days was a luxury that I'd not experienced in the last couple of years. This is not to ignore or belittle the human loss, the personal hardship or the financial pressure of the pandemic, but I was grateful to press the slow-motion button, reset and connect with my family and myself. I think that changed me and is continuing to change me now.

Since life as I knew it was totally disrupted, the new fear became: what does the future look like? The uncertainty was scary, but it also felt like an opportunity. Lockdown gave me the mental space to really focus on what I want to achieve. It made me reframe my vision and decide which things I wanted to put 100 per cent into. So, rather than firing loads of bullets and putting only ten per cent into each of them, I was only going to fire three.

This is the reason that I formally announced my retirement from professional snowboarding in January 2021. Rather than trying to juggle a professional career in snowsports with my broadcast work, I decided I wanted to streamline the vision and put more energy and focus into what I really wanted. At the end of the day, it's a bit like what my dad said when I was younger: you can be average at a lot of things, but you can only be really, really good at one. For a while I was doing both, I'd be interviewed live about some of my broadcast work and I'd get asked: how's the training going for the Olympics? For me with my adapted motto of putting out what you want to achieve and manifesting it into being, having two careers wasn't setting the right foundation for my future goals. Even though they somewhat complemented each other, being a professional snowboarder was taking away from my next calling – becoming the next Clare Balding ;-)

Filming the North Korean documentary for the Olympic Channel had re-enforced that this is what I love to do. I love telling stories of sportspeople, exploring unknown territories, documenting it, and working with a team to bring people at home an immersive and complete experience. I'm not in it for the quick content game. Let's be honest, we all like to digest those easy one-minute clips on socials, but for me the art is being immersed in a project of substance where there's a key takeaway for the viewer. That, to me, is rewarding, and I feel like it's my calling. Post-snowboarding, broadcasting was where I wanted to be, but manifesting that direction is like playing chess – there's no clear route or opportunity put in front of you.

Back at the 2014 Olympics, I had my first experience in the commentary box. Jenny Jones became the first British woman to win a medal on the snow. Imagine one of your best mates and a huge role model clinching a bit of hardware from the biggest event in the world. Let's just say, I didn't hold back on my raw emotions. But let's not forget, I was a snowboarder and not a broadcaster.

It took until the 2018 Winter Olympics for my interest in broadcast to really take hold. I began vlogging the build-up to the games, documenting the lifestyle of an elite athlete, showcasing my training, nutrition and the locations to which my sport had taken me. This then caught the interest of the BBC digital team, who asked me to vlog for them throughout the Games. To most people this would seem like a distraction, but for me it was a positive diversion because it was where my energy and focus had shifted. The power of an event like the Olympics is amazing. I did one video, which went viral. I came out of the Village for two days to see my family in Seoul and I was getting noticed walking around one of the biggest cities in Asia. How did that even happen? Anyway, it didn't faze me and I continued to document my experience, this time with the support of South Korean fans as well as British fans.

After the last day of the competition, I was celebrating with Anna Gasser (who took home the gold medal in the Big Air) at a big party in the Austrian team house. I was letting my hair down, dancing the night away and enjoying the celebrations for what was truly a remarkable performance. Mid-dance, I received a text from a BBC producer asking if I would join Radzi Chinyanganya as a guest the following day for the live broadcast! I immediately started downing water and got my head down for a semi-decent night's sleep so I was fresh-faced and ready to go at 6am in the studio.

That morning totally ignited the fire within me to learn more about this potential new chapter. I grilled the team, I was totally fascinated by broadcasting and that day gave me an opportunity to meet everyone and immerse myself by asking all of the questions and chatting to all the people. I was admiring Radzi's skillset and met a new lifelong friend. Who would have thought it, sat at the bottom of a derelict Olympic slope in South Korea? Clearly the chat wasn't too bad because they asked me back for a second day and it all spiralled from there.

*

Although my introduction to the world of broadcasting had happened with a good dose of serendipity, this path has allowed me to hone my practice of positive thinking and manifestation because I feel that, as soon as I dropped in on my last run in PyeongChang, my energy had shifted to a new focal point. I was done, really done, with competing. And you know what? That's okay. Too many people punish themselves for what they think should or would or could have been. I'm not about that. I was happy and content within myself and that's what deep down life is really about. The next step really was all about manifestation and, without even realizing, I was doing it. By vlogging and putting my video work out there, it attracted the eyes of what I like to call 'the right people'. Lots of people like to talk about engagement on social media these days. As much as it might seem like it, it's not a numbers game, it's about the right eyes and the luck of the algorithm. That's my theory on it anyway!

In media, the saying goes, you're only as good as your last job. Building up my broadcast experience became like a snowball effect. It started with Red Bull TV, then Eurosport, and before I knew it I was rubbing shoulders with Andy Murray and asking him what he had for lunch at the Lawn Tennis Association (in case you're wondering, he went for the lasagne). Amazon Prime, BT Sport, BBC *Ski Sunday* features and BBC *Morning Live* all followed. Each one has been a new lesson for me in honing my craft and stepping up to the challenges of both live and pre-recorded broadcasting.

Then, off the back of a rather long winter in lockdown, in March 2021, I decided I wanted to be my own boss and my own creative, so I came up with the concept of *Monday Mile*. It's essentially a podcast, but it's filmed and it's on the move. We create a visual highlight reel, cut down for social, to entice the viewer to listen. The hook being that the best conversations happen sideways. We had all spent so much time sitting down and locked down, so we needed something different. I thought, *Let's take the conversation outside and away from our screens.* So I started my own podcast.

Monday Mile is all about forward–flowing energy and digging into people's idiosyncrasies, morning routines and inspirational stories as to how they find the motivation to keep excelling in their field. From working with my good friend, producer extraordinaire Tom Mallion, I've learned so much about production, the importance of good audio, and I've been inspired by all of my guests in their own unique ways. The podcast has certainly been immersive to work on and a fundamental building block in establishing my craft, but without my guests it would be nothing. We've had Wayne Bridge dancing to Bob Marley on a football field in Cobham, Jenny Falconer walking her London commute home with us, Katya Jones sharing her views on energy and dancing her way around a park in Shoreditch, Chris Hoy creating awareness around cycling for all, and Dr Ranj talking about the big C word and the topic of mental health.

In another perfect example of the power of manifestation, the success of *Monday Mile* led to *The Olympic Mile*, a 13-part series for BBC Sounds, where I got to chat to some of my favourite faces in the Team GB class of Tokyo 2020. It's mad to think where the sport of snowboarding has taken me, so thank you to each and every one of my guests for sharing your time.

In many ways, my broadcasting career has been a movement away from fear. Don't get me wrong, the focus and adrenaline during a live broadcast is hard to replicate, and it's comparable to that ultimate flow state that I entered in a mountainside performance. In a live broadcast you're so tuned in, so on it, and you absolutely have to get it right first time. It's mentally taxing as opposed to physically taxing. In contrast however, that physical danger, that ultimate fear that blighted some of my biggest snowboarding jumps, is absent...I sigh with relief. And in its place is the total buzz of bouncing ideas off other people, learning, improving and thriving.

There are lots of elements of snowboarding and broadcast that correlate; however performing live adds a different dynamic of pressure. In some ways it's tougher than snowboarding because in snowboarding you get two runs.

For a live broadcast it's just the one, and if that goes wrong that's it. So, aspects of snowboarding have helped my confidence in front of the camera, and I'd definitely say that the most positive experience my snowboarding career has given me is my sense of perspective: I'm safe, I'm not in danger, I can see the bigger picture. That makes me feel more relaxed.

The challenge of this new chapter is that there is no direct path any more. In sport the evolution and progression to being the best is clear: you've got to be faster, stronger and more creative than the riders that went before you. There are incremental hurdles, like competitions, that allow you to separate yourself from the rest. In broadcast, it's not a competition, and believe it or not, I'm actually not competitive. My theory is, you should only be competitive with yourself, and by doing so I want to go out there and perform better than I did yesterday. That's the best I can do. In my career I want to make myself irreplaceable, and I can do that by focusing on the two Ps: perspective and practice. This allows my evolution.

I want to progress so I'm constantly asking myself: *How can I get better? What can I learn from this? Where can I improve?* To do this you need opportunities and these are the hardest things to get, so that's where manifestation comes in. I'm a firm believer that if you put it out there, practise in your own time and visualize your success, that can only further contribute to your life goals. And that's what I'm doing, one step at a time.

17

OWNING YOUR OWN TIME

Now that life is feeling a bit more normal, what I am trying to do is maintain that mental space and not go back to the level of activity I had before the pandemic. A big thing I've learned is the value of time management, avoiding it being a heavy weight on me, because that in itself is stressful; that feeling of, *How on earth am I going to fit it all in?* The challenge for us all is to balance the fear of missing out with making sure we do what we love. Making time for whatever it is that gives us joy, without creating a stressful feeling of over-managing time. You know that feeling of going for a run, when you've not allowed enough time, and you've got to be back in half an hour? A time-pressured run instantly loses the sacred mental space it can take you to.

The secret is to spread things out and take a little more

time to indulge in each activity you invest in. Doing a little less, maybe being more gentle and giving yourself that little bit more time.

So, what is the positive if you end up doing less? Well, we may be taking more time over it, but by actively trying to squeeze in less, we are more present and remove ourselves from the fight-or-flight presence of trying to get too much done in too little time. We will invariably get more pleasure from it. Sometimes, the best path is to say no, because turning down a short-term pleasure will help us to avoid the build-up of long-term stress. We all know that feeling.

The worst feeling in the world is to over-schedule, underperform and be disappointed because we haven't given something proper time. As a freelancer, some days are stacked in comparison to others. That's why if I can't balance my day, I balance my week, and I do that by adding in something that's healthy, that feeds my soul. For me, that's getting out on the boat and wakesurfing with my friends. It's not easy scheduling free time, but it's important to leave little blocks to allow freedom and *ad hoc* decisions, whether it's impromptu coffee with a friend, or a longer catch-up over food. Those are the moments we all treasure and it's impossible if we don't schedule the time.

The wonders of connectivity have given us the illusion of happiness in the swipe of an app. They create the promise of finding love, achieving fitness and managing your nutrition, but these tightly curated visions of the lives of others offered by social media can leave us feeling empty and hollow, rather like eating fast food. There is ample evidence that we increasingly measure ourselves through these airbrushed '#nofilter' images. The question is: are we really living our lives, or are we collecting a series of moments to present on social media? Are you satisfied and sustained by your life, or does it leave you feeling empty and undernourished? I would suggest we should under-schedule to thrive, not over-schedule to survive.

If you have a tendency to push yourself, set goals and strive for constant evolution and progression, then the antidote is perhaps to strive to do less, but make sure it's high quality. If your greatest fear in life is the fear of missing out, then make sure you have a balance. Counter your fear of missing out right now by ring-fencing some time to kill. The biggest lesson is: don't try to fit too much in. Enjoy each thing you do and go for quality rather than quantity in everything. As I have often had cause to note, karma is a bitch. I think what you put out comes back in terms of energy, vibe and work ethic.

It's easy to get distracted by the muffle and the white noise of those around you, and that's why it's so important to surround yourself with people on the same wavelength, with the same life motto, building each other up, supporting each other, and being better than you were yesterday. My openness, my vulnerability, my tendency to overshare sometimes, have previously caught me off guard. But now I try to remove myself from such toxic environments. My awareness and understanding of energy and frequencies has changed substantially and it's something that I'm passionate about now.

*

Since the PyeongChang Olympics in 2018, I've enjoyed the sporadic nature of things, the business of being busy. Now it's time to get back to the basic fundamentals of good routine. One of the biggest challenges I found during the first COVID-19 lockdown was how to keep my mind and body together. Without an event or something to work towards, it was hard for me to channel my energy. I recognized quite early on that if I didn't move first thing in the morning, physically I was going to feel pretty crap. I now get up every day and move first thing, because I know how much energy it gives me. It's all about sticking to the healthy path. If I have a busy day ahead, I will set my alarm an hour earlier so that I can still go and have that walk in the park, that morning coffee, that yoga session, that one thing that sets me up for the day. I've made the first step to guaranteeing I ring-fence some of the best time I will have that day.

If you don't have a consistent routine, life will give you one – and it may not be the one you want. It leaves you vulnerable to being pulled in multiple directions, distracted by different people and random things. If you don't learn from past mistakes or build a healthy practice, if you don't actually stick to your plans, you can be knocked off course and achieve nothing. It might be fun for a minute, or a few days, but that can quickly turn into a week or a week-and-a-half cruising on other people's schedules.

To truly live, rather than exist, you need to own your life and know what your priorities are today and in the future. So, what's the one thing you want to achieve this week, this year, in five years' time? Set your intention now, maintain that focus and, most importantly, enjoy the ride. If you are open to life's opportunities, they will come to you. And if fear has been the thing holding you back, I hope this book has helped you to reframe it. Fear will always be a part of your life, but your perspective, your skills and your routine should be too. Just take a deep breath and put one foot in front of the other. You've got this.

TIMELINE OF KEY DATES

1995
Parents buy first trampoline (which swiftly gets returned!)
A quad bike arrives in the garden.

1996
Quad bike is replaced by a motocross bike.

2001
Masters backflip on a trampoline.

2003
Whole family moves to the USA.

2006
High Cascade Snowboard Camp on Mount Hood, Oregon,
USA.

2007

February: Broken collarbone in Breckenridge, Colorado.

July: High Cascade Snowboard Camp on Mount Hood, Oregon, USA.

August: Whole family moves to Holywood, Northern Ireland.

October: Roxy Future Team Camp, Saas Fee, Switzerland. Offered Roxy sponsorship.

December: Roxy Chicken Jam Competition, Kaprun, Austria.

2008

December: Team GB training and Roxy Freestyle training, Keystone, Colorado, USA. Breaks coccyx.

2009

June: Full-time member of GB Freestyle Team.

September: Enrols at Bath University.

2011

November: Wins O'Neill Pleasure Jam, Dachstein, Austria.

2012

February: Roxy Pro, Saalbach Hinterglemm, Austria.

October: Signs with Red Bull. Trains at Red Bull pre-season camp in New Zealand and completes first double backflip.

November: Wins O'Neill Pleasure Jam, Dachstein, Austria.

December: The Dew Tour, Breckenridge, USA. Completes 2½ backflips and injures rotator cuff with a grade-two tear.

2013

January: World Cup, Copper Mountain, Colorado, USA. Slopestyle Olympic qualifying event.

January: World Championship, Quebec, Canada. Slopestyle Olympic qualifying event. Stands down from event due to injury.

March: X Games, Tignes, France. Becomes first woman to land double backflip in a competition.

July: Training camp in Whistler, Canada. Injures acromioclavicular joint with a grade-two tear.

August: World Cup, Cardrona, New Zealand. Slopestyle Olympic qualifying event.

November: O'Neill Pleasure Jam, Dachstein, Austria.

December: World Cup, Copper Mountain, Colorado, USA. Slopestyle Olympic qualifying event.

2014

February: Winter Olympics, Sochi, Russia. Team GB
member, Slopestyle.

2016

November: World Cup, Milan, Italy. Big Air Olympic
qualifying event.
December: Injures lateral ligament of the ankle with a
grade-two tear.

2017

January: World Cup, Seiser Alm, Italy. Slopestyle Olympic
qualifying event.
February: World Cup, Mammoth Mountain, California,
USA. Slopestyle Olympic qualifying event.
March: World Cup, Špindlerův Mlýn, Czech Republic.
Slopestyle Olympic qualifying event.
September: World Cup, Cardona, New Zealand. Slopestyle
Olympic qualifying event.
December: World Cup, Mönchengladbach, Germany. Big Air
Olympic qualifying event.
Finishes third overall in World Cup Super Series Big Air and
fifth in World Cup Slopestyle.

2018

February: Winter Olympics, PyeongChang, South Korea.
Team GB member, Slopestyle and Big Air.

2019

March–April: Runs Pyongyang Marathon, North Korea and
films the documentary, *Running in North Korea*.

2020

January: Hosts first feature on BBC *Ski Sunday*.

2021

January: Announces retirement from professional
snowboarding.
March: Starts *Monday Mile* podcast series.
July: Creates *The Olympic Mile* BBC Sounds podcast series.

2022

February: BBC pundit for 2022 Winter Olympics, Beijing,
China.

ACKNOWLEDGEMENTS

Thank you to:

- Mum , Dad and Josh.
- Nanny Ot for being my biggest supporter.
- My snowboarding friends for life – Silje Norendal, Jenny Jones, Torah Bright and Jamie Nicholls.
- Lesley McKenna and Alison Robb.
- Radzi Chinyanganya and Tom Mallion.
- And finally to Carl Hindmarch.